SWATZPROJECTZ

TO

OBAN

SCOTLAND

Insider Guide to Oban's Best-Kept Secrets

Orson Noel

COPYRIGHT NOTICE

This publication is copyright protected. This is only for personal use. No part of this publication may be, including but not limited to, reproduced, in any form or medium, stored in a data retrieval system or transmitted by or through any means, without prior written permission from the Author / Publisher.

Legal action will be pursued if this is breached.

DISCLAIMER

Please note that the information contained within this document is for educational purposes only. The information contained herein has been obtained from sources believed to be reliable at the time of publication. The opinions expressed herein are subject to change without notice.

Readers acknowledge that the Author / Publisher is not engaging in rendering legal, financial or professional advice. The Publisher / Author disclaims all warranties as to the accuracy, completeness, or adequacy of such information.

The Publisher assumes no liability for errors, omissions, or inadequacies in the information contained herein or from the interpretations thereof. The publisher / Author specifically disclaims any liability from the use or application of the information contained herein or from the interpretations thereof.

TABLE OF CONTENT

COPYRIGHT NOTICE ii
DISCLAIMER iii
TABLE OF CONTENT iv
INTRODUCTION 1
   Welcome to Oban, Scotland! 1
   About the Travel Guide 2
   Why Oban, Scotland? 7
   How to Use This Guide. 11
CHAPTER 1 16
BEST TIME TO VISIT AND DURATION OF STAY. 16
   Understanding Oban Seasons 16
   Best Weather and Activity Times 18
   Best Time for Events & Festivals 20
   Best Time to Avoid Crowds. 22
   How Long to Stay: Recommended Trip Durations ... 24
Chapter 2 27
GETTING TO OBAN: YOUR TRANSPORTATION OPTIONS 27
   Car Travel: Routes and Parking 27
   Travel by Train: The Scenic West Highland Line 29
   Bus/Coach Transportation: National and Local Services 31
   Flying In: Nearby Airports (Glasgow, Edinburgh) and Beyond Travel 33

Arriving by Sea: Ferry Connections for Non-Tourist Arrivals. 35
Chapter 3 37
ARRIVING IN OBAN: FIRST IMPRESSIONS AND ORIENTATION. 37
   Navigating the Town Center 37
   Visitor Information Center 40
   Important Landmarks for Orientation 43
   Getting Your Bearings: Maps and Applications 46
Chapter 4 50
TRANSPORTATION WITHIN OBAN. 50
   Walking: Exploring Oban by Foot 50
   Local Bus Routes and Schedules 53
   Taxis and Rideshares: Getting Around Easily 54
   Bike Rentals for Eco-Friendly Exploration 56
   Ferries to Nearby Islands: Schedules and Tips 57
   Car Rentals for Navigating the Region 58
   Accessibility Options for Travelers 60
Chapter 5 62
ACCOMMODATION IN OBAN. 62
   Overview of Accommodation Options. 62
   Luxury Resorts. 64
   Budget-Friendly Hotels 65
   Boutique Guesthouses. 67
   Unique Stays (e.g., glamping, historic cottages). 69
   Most Recommended Accommodation 70

Selecting the Suitable Accommodation for You 71
Bookkeeping Tips and Tricks 72

Chapter 6 75
TOP TOURIST ATTRACTIONS. 75
McCaig's Tower: Stunning Views of Oban 75
Oban Distillery: A Taste of Scottish Whisky. 76
Dunollie Castle: History & Heritage 78
Oban War and Peace Museum's Local Stories 79
St. Columba's Cathedral: Architectural Gem. 80
Atlantis Leisure: Family-Friendly Entertainment 81
Ganavan Sands: Scenic Beach Walk 82
Pulpit Hill, Panoramic Lookout Point 83
Oban Phoenix Cinema - Cultural Entertainment 84
Kerrera Island: Day Trip Adventure. 85

CHAPTER 7 87
DINING AT OBAN 87
Seafood Specialties: Fresh from the Harbor 87
Traditional Scottish Cuisine 89
International Dining Options 90
Cafes and Bakeries for Quick Bite 92
Best Restaurants and Hidden Gems 93
Dietary Considerations: Vegan, Gluten-Free, And More 94
Dining Etiquette and Tipping 96

Chapter 8 98
OUTDOOR ACTIVITIES AND ADVENTURES 98

    Hiking Trails Around Oban. 98
    Water Activities: Kayaking, Sailing, and More. 100
    Wildlife Watching: Seals, Birds, and Dolphins. 102
    Fishing trips and charters. 103
    Golfing In Scenic Surroundings 105
    Guided Tours for Outdoor Enthusiasts 106
Chapter 9 109
CULTURAL EXPERIENCES 109
    Local Music and Ceilidhs. 109
    Art Gallery and Craft Shops 111
    Historic Walking Tours 112
    Gaelic Culture and Language Fundamentals 113
    Visiting Local Markets and Fairs. 115
    Engaging in Community Events 116
Chapter 10 119
SOUVENIRS AND SHOPPING: BRINGING OBAN HOME 119
    Independent Shops and Boutiques 119
    Scottish Craft and Woollens 121
    Whiskey and Local Spirits Retailers 123
    Art Gallery and Studio 125
    Food Souvenirs: Smoked Salmon, Cheese and Tablet 126
Chapter 11 129
EXPLORING BEYOND OBAN: POPULAR DAY TRIPS 129

Isle of Mull: Tobermory and Duart Castle. 130
Isle of Iona: Abbey and Spiritual Significance. 131
Isle of Staffa: Fingal's Cave and Puffins (seasonal). ... 132
Island of Kerrera: Walking and History. 134
Kilmartin Glen: Ancient Standing Stones and Cairns 135
Inveraray, Castle and Jail 136
Seil Island and the 'Bridge Over the Atlantic' 137
Plan Your Day Trip 138

Chapter 12 141
NIGHTLIFE AND ENTERTAINMENT 141
Pubs & Bars: Where to unwind 141
Live Music Venues. 143
Theater and Cinema Experiences. 144
Evening Harbor Walks. 146
Seasonal Nightlife Events. 147

Chapter 13 150
SUGGESTED ITINERARIES FOR MAKING THE MOST OF YOUR TIME 150
Weekend Getaway (2-3 Days) 150
Cultural Immersion (4–5 days) 152
Celsius. Outdoor Adventure (5-7 Days) 155
Family-Friendly Trip (4 Days) 157
Budget Travel (3-4 days) 159
Flexible Solo Traveler's Guide 161
Romantic Getaways (3 Days) 163

CHAPTER 14
DO'S AND DONT'S. 165
Must-Dos for a Great Visit 165
Common Mistakes to Avoid 167
Cultural Sensitivity and Etiquette 169
Safety Tips for Travelers 170
Environmental Responsibility 172

Chapter 15 175
PRACTICAL INFORMATION 175
Currency and Payment Options. 175
Internet and Mobile Connectivity 177
Local Time Zone and Business Hours. 178
Healthcare and Medical Services 180
Packing Tip for Oban's Climate 181
Visa & Entry Requirements 183

Chapter 16 185
FAMILY-FRIENDLY ACTIVITIES 185
Child-Friendly Attractions and Museums ... 185
Outdoor Play Spaces and Parks 187
Family Boat Trips & Tours 189
Workshops and Interactive Experiences. 190
Dining Options for Families 192

Chapter 17 194
FESTIVALS AND EVENTS 194
Oban Games: Highland Traditions. 194
West Highland Yachting Week 196

Oban Seafood Festival 197
Winter Festival and Christmas Events 199
Book Tickets and Plan Ahead 200

Chapter 18 204
SUSTAINABLE TRAVEL IN OBAN 204
Eco-Friendly Accommodation and Dining 204
Supporting Local Business 206
Reducing Your Environmental Impact 207
Volunteering and Community Initiatives. 209
Green Transport Options 211

Chapter 19 213
PLAN YOUR TRIP 213
Making a Personalized Itinerary 213
Book Tours and Activities 215
Travel Insurance and Safety 217
Packing Checklist 218
Final Tips for a Memorable Stay 220

APPENDIX: YOUR ESSENTIAL OBAN TOOLKIT 222
Emergency Contacts. 222
Maps and Navigational Tools. 224
Map of Oban 226
Map of Things to Do 227
Map of Museums 228
Map of Transit Stations 229
Map of Hiking Trails 230

Map of ATMs 231
Map of Hotels 232
Map of Restaurants 233
Map of Vacation Rentals 234
Additional Reading and References 235
Useful Local Phrases... 236
Addresses and Locations for Popular Accommodation 237
Addresses and Locations for Popular Restaurants and Cafes... 239
Addresses and Locations for Popular Bars and Clubs... 240
Addresses And Locations of Major Attractions 241
Addresses And Locations of Bookstore 243
Addresses And Locations of Leading Clinics, Hospitals, And Pharmacies... 244
Addresses and locations of UNESCO World Heritage Sites 245

INTRODUCTION

Welcome to Oban, Scotland!

Hello, and a very warm Scottish welcome (or fàilte, as we often say!) to Oban!

Imagine a lively, horseshoe-shaped bay teeming with boats, ranging from little fishing boats to magnificent CalMac ferries waiting to whisk you away to lovely islands. Picture colorful houses clustered around the shoreline, guarded by a somewhat unique, Colosseum-like monument positioned high on a hill. Hear the screams of seagulls mix with the cheery buzz of taverns and seafood shacks. Smell the distinct, revitalizing salty sea air, blended with the faint, sweet aroma of whiskey mash from the nearby distillery.

My friend, that is your first taste of Oban.

Oban, located on Scotland's gorgeous west coast in the Argyll and Bute region, is more than a town; it is an experience. It's affectionately known as the "Gateway to the Isles" because it serves as the primary ferry hub linking the mainland to the Hebridean islands of Mull, Iona, Staffa, and beyond. It is also proudly and deservedly called the "Seafood Capital of Scotland." Hope your taste buds are ready for this!

Oban has a way of capturing your heart, whether you're standing on the dock watching the boats come in, strolling the lovely alleyways, hiking up for the renowned view from McCaig's Tower, or simply savoring the best seafood you've ever eaten. It's a location where beautiful landscapes meet dynamic town life, and ancient historical significance coexists with modern adventures.

So, unpack your baggage, take a deep breath of the fresh sea air, and prepare to explore. You've arrived in Oban, where an exciting voyage awaits.

About the Travel Guide

Okay, let's talk about the book you're holding. Trust this guide to be your pleasant and knowledgeable companion as you explore everything Oban has to offer. We've poured over maps, talked to locals, tried (perhaps too much!) amazing cuisine, toured castles, jumped on ferries, and generally laid the foundation so you can spend less time worried and more time enjoying your precious holiday.

Who Is This Guide For?

Honestly? This is for you. Whether you are:

A First-Time Visitor: wide-eyed and unsure where to begin (don't worry, we have you covered!).

A Seasoned Oban Enthusiast: Returning for another dose of west coast charm and maybe seeking for any hidden jewels you missed the last time.

Part Of a Tour Group: Want to make the most of your leisure time or learn more about the places you're visiting.

On a Family Vacation: Looking for activities that will keep everyone pleased, from toddlers to grandparents.

A Solo Adventurer: looking for tips on traveling Oban securely and making connections.

A Couple on a Romantic Getaway: Looking for gorgeous places and cozy corners.

An Outdoor Enthusiast: Ready to hike, kayak, or simply enjoy the breathtaking scenery.

A Foodie: Anxious to get into the famed seafood scene.

Basically, if Oban is on your radar, this book will help you plan, explore, and fall in love with the town.

What's Inside?

We've made an effort to include everything you'll need for a satisfying, enjoyable, and stress-free journey. Inside these pages, you will discover:

Inspiration: Helping you figure out why Oban should be on your list (Even if we believe it sells itself!).

Planning Essentials: Information on the ideal times to travel, how long to stay, and how to get here.

Accommodation Advice: From luxurious hotels to low-cost B&Bs and unique self-catering options, we'll help you locate the ideal base.

Getting Around: Useful tips on traversing Oban and using it as a starting point for further exploration (hello, ferries!).

Must-See Attractions: We highlight the best views, from the landmark McCaig's Tower and the ancient Oban Distillery to lesser-known local favorites.

Food: Where to get the best seafood, cozy cafés, traditional pub fare, and, of course, a tiny dram of whiskey.

Activities Galore: There are several activities available, including boat cruises, animal watching, hiking, shopping, cultural experiences, and soaking up the local vibe.

Island Hopping and Day Trips: Information on visiting the beautiful neighboring islands and mainland attractions that are easily accessible from Oban.

Practicalities: Important information on money, safety, health, keeping connected, and even dealing with bothersome midges!

Local Knowledge: Tips on etiquette ("Do's and Don'ts"), knowing local culture, and finding valuable services.

Suggested Itineraries: Ready-made plans for a variety of trip lengths and interests to get you started.

Quick Reference: A helpful appendix with maps, emergency contacts, useful addresses, and more.

Our Approach: We think travel should be pleasurable and not overwhelming. So, we strove for a conversational, easy-to-read style. While we strive for authenticity and comprehensive coverage of the highlights, this is not an encyclopedia that lists every single store or bed and breakfast. Instead, it's a curated guide that focuses on great experiences and practical advice to help you get the most out of your trip. We want this book to feel more like a buddy giving you advice on Oban than like a textbook.

Consider this guide to be your launchpad. It provides information and inspiration, but the true magic happens when you go out and explore Oban for yourself. Let's get started.

WHY OBAN, SCOTLAND?

So, with so many beautiful destinations to visit in Scotland (and throughout the world), why would you choose Oban? What makes this specific location on the west coast so unique? Of course, lets count the ways! Oban is beyond mere stopover; it's a destination with its own distinct charm and a perfect blend of experiences.

It Really Is the "Gateway to the Isles":

This is beyond a simple catchy phrase. Oban's harbor is the hub of Caledonian MacBrayne's (or CalMac, as they are known) ferry services to the Inner and Outer Hebrides. Standing on the dock, seeing these historic vessels come and go, creates an authentic sense of adventure. Want to explore the vibrant port town of Tobermory on Mull? Would you like to visit the hallowed Isle of Iona? Admire the geological wonder of Fingal's Cave on Staffa. See the Islay whisky distilleries? Oban is the crucial starting spot. The simplicity with which you can board a ferry for a day excursion or a longer island tour is a big plus.

The Seafood Capital of Scotland: No Exaggeration!

If you enjoy seafood, welcome to paradise. Oban's harborside is studded with outlets offering the freshest catch possible, often directly from the boat. From rustic seafood shacks on the pier serving famed prawn sandwiches, oysters, and scallops to wonderful restaurants serving gourmet fish meals, the quality and variety are exceptional. Imagine plump mussels boiled in white wine, luscious langoustines grilled with garlic butter, perfectly cooked scallops, and exquisite smoked salmon... it's a foodie's dream come true. Even if you don't typically like fish, Oban could just make you a sea food lover!

Natural Beauty: Oban offers breathtaking scenery. The village wraps around a protected cove with stunning views of the Isle of Kerrera and Mull's distant highlands. Climb to McCaig's Tower (you can't miss it!) for breathtaking panoramic views, particularly around sunset. Take a stroll along the Esplanade, visit neighboring Ganavan Sands beach, or travel a little farther afield for stunning coastline treks and tranquil lochs. The interaction of water, islands, hills, and the attractive town itself results in a visual feast.

Oban's Rich History and Culture: Explore the remains of Dunollie Castle, the historic seat of the Clan MacDougall that stands spectacularly above the bay entrance. Discover how the town grew rapidly throughout the Victorian era, fueled by the entrance of the railway and steamships. The Oban War & Peace Museum showcases local history. And, of course, there's the Oban Distillery, one of Scotland's oldest, located right in the middle of town; a tour provides an intriguing view into the history and technique of whiskey production. The town's fabric also includes remnants of Gaelic culture and a strong nautical history.

A Vibrant Yet Relaxed Atmosphere:

Oban has a vibrant yet relaxed atmosphere. There's a palpable excitement in the waterfront and town center, especially during high season, with visitors coming and going, shops perusing, and diners enjoying local cuisine.

However, it maintains a friendly, inviting small-town atmosphere. The locals are typically kind, and there is a good pace of life. You might easily spend hours roaming around, watching the world go by, or stopping at a nice bar for a pint and a talk.

Basecamp for Adventure:

Oban is an ideal location for visiting the Argyll region, beyond just the town and its islands. You're close to the prehistoric wonders of Kilmartin Glen, the fairytale castle at Inveraray, the dramatic landscapes of Glencoe (a little further, but doable), and countless opportunities for hiking, cycling, kayaking, wildlife watching (seals, otters, sea eagles, and even whales!), and simply immersing yourself in nature.

It's Accessible:

Oban is easily accessible, unlike other isolated Highlands and Islands. It is connected to Glasgow by a picturesque railway line (the West Highland Line - an adventure in itself!), strong road connections, and frequent bus services. This makes it a viable location for both short trips and extended vacations.

In essence, Oban offers a compelling package that includes spectacular landscape, amazing food, easy access to legendary islands, a deep history, a friendly mood, and lots of adventure. It's a destination that caters to a variety of preferences and creates an indelible impact. Are you convinced yet? We thought so!

How to Use This Guide.

Okay, so you've got this guide, you're enthusiastic about Oban, and you're ready to plan, or you're already here and don't know where to start. How can you get the most out of this book? Here are some friendly suggestions:

Do Not Treat It As A Strict Rulebook.

Think of this guide as a buffet rather than a set menu. Dip in and out. Read the chapters that interest you the most. Skip the parts that are not relevant to your trip. Your Oban adventure is entirely up to you, and this guide is intended to help you shape it rather than prescribe it. Feel free to mix and match our ideas, explore your own interests, and become delightfully distracted; sometimes the finest discoveries happen unexpectedly!

For the Planning Phase (Before You Leave):

If you're still in the planning stages, these chapters will be very helpful right now:

Chapter 3 (Best Time to Visit & Duration): Provides guide on when and how long to visit based on your priorities (weather, crowds, and events).

Chapter 4 (Getting to Oban): Essential for determining your journey logistics: vehicle, rail, or bus?

Chapter 7 (Where to Stay): Essential reading for locating and reserving your lodging base. Before making a decision, look over your alternatives and tips.

Chapter 13 (Suggested Itineraries): An excellent resource for getting ideas and seeing how you may plan your days, even if you change them later. Examine the many themes (weekend, adventure, family, etc.) to discover what resonates.

On the Ground (During Your Visit):

Once you are in Oban, this additional chapters will become your go-to resources:

Chapters 5 (Arriving and Orientation) and 6 (Getting Around) will help you gain your bearings and find out how to navigate the town and local transportation.

Chapter 8 (Top Ten Attractions): Your checklist of must-see sites.

Chapter 9 (A Taste of Oban): When hunger strikes, use this guide to identify the greatest seafood, cafés, pubs, and restaurants.

Chapters 10 (Activities & Experiences) and 11 (Outdoor Enthusiasts) include ideas for activities ranging from boat cruises to walks.

Chapter 14 (Day Trips) is essential if you're planning trips to the islands or adjacent mainland destinations. Check the ferry timings shown below, but always double-check official sources!

Oban After Dark: Ideas for evening amusement.

The Appendix: Keep this handy for rapid lookups of emergency numbers, locations, and map resources.

Use Structure: We've organized information into chapters and subtopics (e.g., 1.1, 1.2) to make it easier to find. Use the Table of Contents at the beginning to easily get to the section you want. The subheadings inside each chapter should also assist you in searching for specific facts.

Look for Tips and Insights: Our guide includes practical tips, local insights, and information to enhance your trip experience. Keep a look out for them!

Integrate with Other Resources: Although we attempted to be comprehensive, things can change! Always double-check operating hours, ferry timetables (very important!) and costs on official websites or by contacting beforehand, especially outside of the peak summer season. Use online map apps in addition to the map resources we provide. Speak with the workers at the local Visitor Information Centre; they are fountains of knowledge!

Personalize It: Add notes in the margins! Highlight areas that interest you. Fold down the page corners. Use sticky notes. As you engage with this guide, it will become more useful as your own Oban planner.

Most Importantly, Explore And Enjoy!

Use this guide as a springboard, then set it aside and enjoy everything around you. Talk with the locals (they're quite friendly!), go down charming-looking side streets, linger over a coffee or a pint, and savor the moments.

Wrapping Up

Oban is an awesome destination, and we sincerely hope that our guide helps you have an amazing time exploring it. Enjoy your travels!

CHAPTER 1

BEST TIME TO VISIT AND DURATION OF STAY.

So, you're thinking about Oban's waterfront views and seafood feasts? A fantastic thought indeed! But, before you book your flights or rail tickets, let's talk about timing. Oban, like the rest of Scotland, is known for its unpredictable weather. Choosing a suitable season and determining how long you need to take it all in can make a significant difference in your experience.

UNDERSTANDING OBAN SEASONS

Oban's weather is like a Scottish folk song: unpredictable, melancholy, and always enthralling. Oban, located on Scotland's west coast, experiences a marine climate, which includes warm temperatures, lots of rain, and the odd brilliant flash of sunlight. Here's an overview of what each season delivers, so you may choose the feel that best matches you.

Spring (March–May): Spring in Oban is like a new beginning. Temperatures range between 5°C and 12°C (41°F and 54°F), with blossoming wildflowers and calmer streets. Rain is still a frequent visitor, but you'll get crisp, clear days ideal for trekking or climbing McCaig's Tower. It's an ideal time for budget tourists because rates are cheaper before the summer surge.

Summer (June to August): This is the star of the show, with temperatures ranging from 12°C to 18°C (54°F to 64°F) and extended daylight hours, imagine sunsets beyond 10 p.m. It's peak season, so anticipate crowded boats, lively pubs, and outdoor activities such as kayaking or island hopping to Mull. Rain is less common, so bring a waterproof jacket just in case.

Autumn (September to November): Oban is painted in flaming reds and golds, as temperatures drop from 10°C to 5°C (50°F to 41°F). The throngs thin away, making it ideal for intimate pub visits or picturesque drives to Glencoe. Rain falls more often, particularly in

November, yet the dark skies give drama to your photographs.

Winter (December-February): Winter is peaceful and comfortable, with temperatures ranging from 2°C to 7°C (36°F to 45°F). Rain is more prevalent than snow on the slopes. It's ideal for visiting interior attractions like the Oban Distillery or relaxing with a whiskey by a fire. Holiday markets and winter events offer a joyful atmosphere.

Each season has its own appeal, so your option is based on your preferences; sunny hikes, celebratory moods, or a calm vacation. Let's break it down further to suit your travel preferences.

Best Weather and Activity Times

If you're organizing your Oban vacation around weather and activities, summer (June to August) is your best choice, but other seasons offer their own advantages. Here's how to coordinate your plans with Mother Nature.

Summer for Outdoor Fun: Summer's mild temperatures and long days make it an ideal season for outdoor activities. Hike to Pulpit Hill for breathtaking vistas, kayak along the shore, or catch a ferry to Kerrera for a picnic. The ocean is calm (enough), and beaches such as Ganavan Sands are ideal for a walk. Just keep in mind that popular attractions like Dunollie Castle can fill up quickly, so book tours in advance.

Spring For Nature Lovers: Spring's lower temperatures and blossoming landscapes are ideal for hikers and photographers. Trails near Loch Etive are less popular, and you may see seals or otters. The weather is unpredictable sun one minute, rain the next—so bring clothes and sturdy footwear.

Autumn for Amazing Beauty: The cool air and bright foliage make it a perfect time for beautiful drives or hikes. Visit Glencoe for breathtaking scenery or stroll Oban's waterfront after sunset. The weather is cooler, but rain is more common, thus indoor alternatives such as the Oban War and Peace Museum are useful.

Winter For Cozy Vibes: Winter is chilly and humid, but it's ideal for indoor activities. Explore the Oban Distillery, see a movie at the Phoenix Cinema, or relax at a bar with live music. If you're lucky, clear days will provide beautiful vistas of snow-capped slopes, ideal for a brief trek with adequate clothing.

Oban's weather, regardless of season, could shift faster than you can say "haggis." Always bring a raincoat, comfortable shoes, and a spirit of exploration. Check the forecast a week before your travel, but don't worry—Oban's beauty shines through rain or shine.

Best Time for Events & Festivals

Oban's calendar is full with events that bring the town to life. Timing your visit around a festival might add a touch of local culture to your vacation. Here are the highlights to plan around.

Summer Festivals (June-August): Summer festival center. The Oban Games in August are a Highland tradition, featuring pipers, dancers, and athletes displaying Scottish patriotism. West Highland Yachting Week (late July/early August) floods the port with sailboats and festivities. These events draw large people, so book your accommodations early.

Autumn Foodie Heaven (September): Foodies should not miss the Oban Seafood Festival in September. Pair fresh scallops, oysters, and more with local whiskey. It's less crowded than in the summer, but restaurants fill up quickly, so make reservations in advance.

Winter Festivities (December): Winter comes the Oban Winter Festival in November/December, which includes Christmas markets, light displays, and warm festivities. It's a beautiful time to drink hot toddies and browse for locally made items. Smaller events, such as Burns Night in January, honor Scottish culture via poetry and haggis.

Spring for Quiet Events (March–May): Spring is calmer, although you can see lesser events like local music evenings or artisan fairs. Check the Oban community calendar closer to your trip for any pop-up activities.

Check Oban's tourism website or social media a few months in advance to see when these activities will take place. Festivals frequently result in increased pricing and overbooked hotels, so book early to get bargains and spaces.

Best Time to Avoid Crowds.

Do you enjoy a tranquil getaway? Oban may be bustling, especially in the summer, but there are some lovely areas for peaceful excursions. Here's how to avoid the crowds and yet enjoy the town's beauty.

Spring (March to May): Usually the ideal time to visit if you want to avoid crowds. Attractions like McCaig's Tower are less crowded, while ferries to the Isles have shorter lineups. April is very tranquil, with nice weather and cheap pricing. Just avoid Easter weekend, since families may come in for short getaways.

Autumn (September-October): Early fall, particularly September, is another crowd-free period. The summer rush has subsided, but the weather is still suitable for outdoor activities. You'll have the trails and beaches of

Ganavan Sands almost to yourself. November becomes rainier, so stay in early October for the finest balance.

Winter (January-February): Winter is the quietest season, ideal for introverts and couples seeking isolation. Pubs and museums are comfortable without being crowded, and you can explore Oban's charm at your own leisure. The Christmas celebrations in December attract some people, so choose for January or February for maximum peace.

Tips For Busy Seasons:

If you're coming during the summer, go early or late (June or August) to avoid the peak July crowds. Visit attractions like Dunollie Castle early in the morning or late in the afternoon, and reserve ferries or excursions ahead of time to avoid long lines.

During quiet seasons, certain attractions and restaurants may have shorter hours, so double-check timetables. What about the trade-off? You'll feel like Oban is your own personal secret.

How Long to Stay: Recommended Trip Durations

How long should you stay in Oban? It depends on your travel style and what you want to fit in. Here's a guide to trip durations, ranging from brief getaways to lengthy explorations.

Weekend Getaway (2–3 Days): A weekend is ideal for a taste of Oban. Spend one day visiting the town, including McCaig's Tower, the distillery, and a seafood feast. Day two, take a ferry to Kerrera or Mull for a brief island experience. It's cramped yet manageable for busy tourists. Ideal for couples and single travelers.

Short Break (4-5 days): Four or five days allow you to explore town and beyond. Spend two days in Oban exploring attractions such as Dunollie Castle and Ganavan Sands, as well as enjoying a cultural night at a ceilidh. Use the remaining days for day trips to Iona or Glencoe. Ideal for families or budget travelers seeking variety.

Week-Long Adventure (7 days): Most people find a week to be the ideal length. You may spend three days in Oban exploring history, gastronomy, and local culture. Use the remaining time to see Mull, Iona, and Staffa islands, as well as a journey to Fort William on the mainland. Ideal for outdoor enthusiasts and cultural junkies.

Extended Stay (10+ days): Do you have any spare time? Ten days or more allows you to live like a native. Spend a week in Oban before spending a few days on an island like Mull or exploring farther afield. Ideal for retirees, digital nomads, and return visitors seeking depth.

Pro Tip: Allow for one additional day in case of weather disruptions; rain may cause plans to change. If you're on a tour, see how much free time you have in Oban to arrange extra activities. Chapter 8's itineraries might help you plan your days.

Wrapping Up

No matter how long you stay, Oban has a way of making you wish you had just a little bit longer time to stay. Choose the duration that best matches your style and priorities, and get set for an unforgettable Scottish west coast adventure!

Chapter 2

GETTING TO OBAN: YOUR TRANSPORTATION OPTIONS

Alright, adventurer, you're ready to head to Oban, Scotland the coastal treasure that's calling at you! Whether you like to travel by car, train, or plane, getting to Oban is half of the pleasure. This chapter is your guide to arriving in style, including information on cars, trains, buses, airlines, and even ferries. Let us go over your options so you can get started right away. Ready? Let's go!

Car Travel: Routes and Parking

If you enjoy the freedom of the open road, traveling to Oban is a pleasure. The routes are picturesque, the sights are stunning, and you can stop for a snap photo whenever inspiration strikes. Oban is around 100 miles northwest of Glasgow, making it a bearable distance from Scotland's major cities.

From Glasgow: The most common route is the A82 to Tyndrum, followed by the A85 straight to Oban. It takes roughly 2.5 hours to travel across Loch Lomond's shoreline and past the majestic peaks of Glen Coe. The roads are well-maintained, although they might be narrow, so take it slowly if you're not used to Scottish driving. Stop at the Green Welly and the Tyndrum for a coffee and a snack, It's a local favorite.

From Edinburgh: Take the M9 to Stirling, then the A84 and A85 to Callander and Crianlarich, which will take around three hours. This route is stunning, with undulating hills and views of the Highlands. It's a little longer, but ideal for soaking up Scotland's panoramas.

From Inverness: Traveling from the north? Take the A82 south through Fort William and then the A828 to Oban. It takes around 2.5 hours, with stunning views of Loch Ness and Ben Nevis along the route.

Park in Oban: Parking is easy once you arrive, however it might be difficult during the summer. The Longsdale Car Park in the town center is your best option for all-day parking (about £5 per day). Street parking is accessible but restricted, with 1–2-hour limits. whether you're staying at a hotel, see whether they provide parking—some do, but spaces fill up quickly. Download the RingGo app for convenient pay-and-display parking.

Tips: If you're planning day trips to Glencoe or Mull, rent a car; nonetheless, most sites in Oban are walkable. Keep an eye out for narrow roads and sheep crossings, and fuel up before leaving larger cities, fuel stations are few in rural areas. Oh, and bring refreshments for those gorgeous stops; you'll want to linger.

Travel by Train: The Scenic West Highland Line

Train enthusiasts, this one is for you. The West Highland Line to Oban is one of the world's most magnificent rail rides, and it's as much about the route as the destination. You'll glide by lochs, mountains, and glens, with views that will have you glued to your window.

From Glasgow: ScotRail operates direct trains from Glasgow Queen Street to Oban, which takes around 3 hours. Expect three to four daily departures, with fares starting at £20 if booked early. The route goes through Crianlarich and Dalmally, offering breathtaking views of Loch Awe and Ben Cruachan. Choose a window seat on the right for the best views.

From Edinburgh: There are no direct trains, however you can connect at Glasgow. Take a 50-minute train ride from Edinburgh Waverley to Glasgow Queen Street before boarding the Oban train. Total trip duration is around 4-8.5 hours. Book both legs on ScotRail's website for a simpler transfer.

From Other Cities: Coming from Inverness or Aberdeen? You'll probably change in Glasgow or Stirling. Check Trainline or ScotRail for schedules, and if you're an international tourist planning several rail travels, consider purchasing a BritRail pass.

In Oban, the train station is located in the town center, just steps away from the harbor and hotels. It's modest, with limited services, so don't anticipate a large center. Taxis and buses are available outside, although most attractions are within walking distance.

Insider Tips: For reduced fares, book tickets 8-12 weeks in advance. Bring a camera the sights are Instagram-worthy. Trains might get crowded throughout the summer, so reserve a seat to ensure availability. If you are prone to motion sickness, the twisting tracks may challenge you, so bring some ginger treats.

Bus/Coach Transportation: National and Local Services

On a budget or simply like a good bus ride? Coaches to Oban are inexpensive and surprisingly comfortable, with services linking major cities and rural communities.

From Glasgow: Scottish Citylink offers frequent buses (Service 975/976) from Buchanan Bus Station to Oban, which takes around 3 hours. Tickets start at £15 one way and take you around Loch Lomond and Tyndrum. Buses include Wi-Fi and charging connections, allowing you to stay connected.

From Edinburgh: Citylink's Service 913 links Edinburgh to Oban via Glasgow, taking approximately 8.5 hours. It takes somewhat longer but is more picturesque, with fares starting at £20. Alternatively, take a speedier bus to Glasgow then transfer to the Oban service.

From Inverness: Citylink's Service 919 travels from Inverness to Oban via Fort William in approximately 3.5 hours. It's a terrific alternative for touring the Highlands, with fares beginning at £18.

Local Buses: West Coast Motors operates local buses that connect Oban to neighboring towns like as Fort William and Campbeltown. These are useful for day trips or if you are staying outside Oban. Schedules vary, so check online or at the Oban bus station.

In Oban: The bus terminal is close to the train station, so you can easily stroll to your hotel or the harbor. On Sundays, buses are less frequent, so plan ahead.

Insider Tips: Book Citylink tickets online for discount offers and arrive 10 minutes early as buses follow schedules. Pack a book or podcast for the journey, and a light jacket for air-conditioned coaches. If you are prone to queasiness, the curving roads may be difficult, so seat near the front.

Flying In: Nearby Airports (Glasgow, Edinburgh) and Beyond Travel

Flying to Oban? There is no airport in town, but Glasgow and Edinburgh provide convenient onward connections.

Glasgow International Airport (GLA): The closest major airport, located around 90 miles from Oban. Flights from London take 1.5 hours, with international connections connecting through hubs such as Dublin or Amsterdam. From GLA, hire a vehicle (2.5-hour drive via A82/A85), take a Citylink bus (3 hours, £20), or take a train from Glasgow Queen Street. Taxis to Oban are expensive (£150 or more), so take public transportation unless you want to splurge.

Edinburgh Airport (EDI): 120 miles distant and better for some international flights. Flights from the United States and Europe are regular, and Oban is a three-hour drive away by M9/A87. Citylink buses (8.5 hours, £20) and trains via Glasgow (8.5 hours, £25) are your best options. Car rentals are generally available, but book early in the summer.

Onward Travel Tips: Both airports have adequate signage for buses and trains. Citylink buses depart from Glasgow's Buchanan Bus Station or Edinburgh's bus depot; airport shuttles will transport you there. For trains, take the airport tram (Edinburgh) or bus (Glasgow) to the city center stations. If you're feeling jet-lagged, try staying overnight in Glasgow or Edinburgh to break up the drive.

Insider Tips: Use Skyscanner to find flight deals, and schedule onward transportation with your flight to save time. Glasgow is closer, but Edinburgh may offer cheaper airfares, so compare them. Pack light for public transportation, lugging baggage on buses is not fun.

Arriving by Sea: Ferry Connections for Non-Tourist Arrivals.

If you're already in the Hebrides or close, coming by ferry is a unique way to get to Oban. These are non-tourist ferries, which means they provide regular services for residents rather than sightseeing trips.

From the Isles: CalMac Ferries connects Oban with Mull, Barra, and South Uist. Oban is about a 50-minute journey from Craignure (Mull), with fares starting at £8. Services from Barra or Lochboisdale are longer (4-5 hours), but more picturesque, and cost between £15 and £20. Check CalMac's website for timetables, since schedules are affected by tides and weather.

Ferries dock at Oban's main terminal, which is located in the town center. You'll arrive within walking distance of hotels, pubs, and the train station. Taxis are provided for anyone arriving late or with heavy luggage.

Insider Tips: Book ferry tickets online, especially in the summer, when vehicles and people fill up quickly. Weather might cause delays in sailings, so prepare a backup plan. Bring a jacket as the deck is windy, but ideal for watching seals.

Wrapping Up

There you have it your guide to getting to Oban, no matter how you travel. Choose your style: picturesque train, low-cost bus, or a road journey with Highland vistas. What are your plans for arriving via ferry or sailing the A85? Let's keep the journey going!

Chapter 3

ARRIVING IN OBAN: FIRST IMPRESSIONS AND ORIENTATION.

Welcome to Oban; you made it! As you enter this quaint Scottish coastal town, the saline breeze, colorful harbor, and hustle of local life will hit you like a warm Highland hug. Whether you arrived by rail, car, or boat, your first moments in Oban are spent soaking up the atmosphere and finding your bearings. This chapter is your helpful guide to navigating the town center, discovering vital resources, identifying landmarks, and using maps or apps to quickly feel like a local. Let's start your Oban trip with wide eyes and a huge smile!

NAVIGATING THE TOWN CENTER

Imagine you're standing in the middle of Oban, with the beautiful Firth of Lorn on one side and the hilly streets leading up to McCaig's Tower on the other. The town center is small, accessible, and full of character, making it simple to explore even if you're new here. To help you hit the ground running, let's go over how to navigate this bustling metropolis.

The Layout: Oban's town core revolves on the waterfront, with the harbor and ferry terminal serving as the primary anchors. The main street, George Street, runs parallel to the sea shore and is dotted with stores, cafés, and taverns. It's the town's heartbeat, filled with both locals and visitors. Smaller roads off George Street, such as Stafford Street and Argyll Square, link to restaurants, hotels, and attractions. Uphill, residential streets lead to landmarks such as McCaig's Tower, providing breathtaking vistas but a bit of a workout.

Getting Around on Foot: Good news: Oban's center is quite pedestrian-friendly. The stroll from the train station to the ferry port takes around 5 minutes, and most attractions, such as the Oban Distillery and St. Columba's Cathedral, are only a 10-minute walk away. The walkways along the main streets are flat, however certain uphill approaches (such as those leading to McCaig's Tower) can be steep. Wear comfortable shoes, especially if you're venturing outside the harbor, and watch out for uneven cobblestones in older sections.

Key Areas to Know:

The Harbor: This is where the action happens, with ferries docked, fishing boats bobbing, and seafood shacks providing fresh catch. It's a nice spot for a coffee and a view to start the day.

North Pier: Located just north of the main harbor, this area features numerous restaurants as well as the touristic rush of gift shops. It's also where you'll locate the iconic Oban sign, ideal for a quick selfie.

Argyll Square: A small square off George Street that houses the bus terminal and serves as a convenient meeting location. It's flanked by eateries and near the train station.

George Street: This is your go-to for shopping, restaurants, and people-watching. Look for landmarks such as the Oban Chocolate Company for a tasty stopover.

Tips for Navigating: Oban's smallness ensures you won't get lost for long, although summer crowds can make the harbor area feel frantic. To avoid tourist traffic, stay on the right side of the sidewalk and use crosswalks at popular areas like the North Pier. If you want mobility assistance, the majority of the town center is accessible; nevertheless, check with your lodging for step-free approaches to hilly sites. Oh, and don't be afraid to ask people for directions, Obanites are very hospitable and like sharing their hometown.

What is your first impression of the town center? It's bustling but relaxed, with the type of charm that makes you want to stay. Grab a fish and chips from a harbor vendor, listen to the gulls, and let Oban's charm take over.

Visitor Information Center

Need some assistance getting started? The Oban Visitor Information Centre is now your best buddy. This hub, located ideally in the town center, is stocked with resources, helpful personnel, and all the insider tips you need to start your vacation like a pro.

Where To Find It: The Visitor Information Centre is located at 3 North Pier, directly on the harbor and only a 3-minute walk from the train station or ferry terminal. Look for the bright blue "I" sign; you won't miss it. It is open year-round, from 9 a.m. to 5 p.m. (longer hours in summer, shorter in winter), but check the VisitScotland website for precise times before visiting.

What's On Offer:

Free Maps and Guides: Pick up a detailed town map, boat schedules, and brochures for Dunollie Castle and day tours to Mull. They also provide guides for surrounding hiking trails and wildlife trips.

Local Advice: The crew are Oban specialists who can answer inquiries like "Where's the best seafood?" and "How do I get to Kerrera?" They can recommend hidden treasures or last-minute activities depending on your preferences.

Bookkeeping Services: Need a tour, a ferry ticket, or lodging? They may assist you with booking guided tours, boat cruises, or even a lodging if you're visiting on the spur of the moment.

Souvenirs & Essentials: Get postcards, local crafts, or useful products like rain ponchos (you are in Scotland, after all!).

Why Should You Visit? Even if you're the sort to plan everything, the center is worth a visit. You could find a pop-up event, such as a local music night, or tips on how to avoid crowds at a popular spot. It's also a fantastic location to recover if you're feeling overwhelmed by options, consider it your Oban HQ.

Tips: Stop by as soon as you arrive to get a map and inquire about current events or weather updates. If you visit during peak season (July-August), expect a short line, although the personnel are efficient. Bring a notepad to write down recommendations, and don't forget to inquire about attraction discounts, some offer unique prices to the center.

Important Landmarks for Orientation

Oban's small size makes it easy to navigate, but a few notable landmarks will help you keep oriented and provide a feel of the town's layout. These renowned sites are like Oban's North Stars; use them to anchor your travels and wow your travel companions with your local knowledge.

McCaig's Tower: This Colosseum-like edifice, perched on a hill overlooking the town, is Oban's most visible feature. It can be seen from practically anywhere in the center, making it an ideal reference point. It's a 10-minute hike upward from George Street, but the views from the top of the harbor, islands, and beyond are worth it. Use it to figure out where you are: if you're facing the tower, the harbor is behind you.

Oban Harbor and Ferry Terminal: The harbor is the focal point of Oban, with the ferry terminal serving as a busy the hub. It is the departure point for CalMac boats to the Isles, and it is often busy. If you're near the water and see ferries or fishing boats, you're in the town center.

The clock tower in the station serves as a convenient meeting point for friends.

St. Columba's Cathedral: This beautiful Gothic church with a lofty steeple is located on the waterfront along Corran Esplanade, just north of the main harbor. It's an excellent marker at the northern edge of the town center. If you spot its stone front while walking, you'll be near to calmer eateries and the way to Ganavan Sands.

Oban Distillery: Located in the heart of town on Stafford Street, this old whisky distillery is both a must-see and a handy landmark. It's located just off George Street, in Argyll Square, so if you visit the distillery, you'll be right in the heart of the retail and dining action.

The North Pier Sign: A colorful "Oban" sign can be found on the North Pier and is a popular photo location. It symbolizes the spot where George Street and the pier meet, and there are restaurants and souvenir stores nearby. If you're at the sign, you're at the most active portion of the waterfront.

How to Use them: Keep an eye out for these landmarks to help you remain on track while you travel. For example, if you're traveling to a restaurant on George Street and see McCaig's Tower ahead, you're on the correct track. If you're near St. Columba's and want to go to the ferry port, head south down the esplanade. These locations also serve as excellent meeting spots, telling someone to "meet me at the Oban sign" is much more convenient than trying to remember street addresses.

Insider Tips: Take a mental picture of where these landmarks are in relation to one another. The harbor serves as your starting point, the distillery is in the center, and the tower is upwards. If you're wandering at night, McCaig's Tower is illuminated, serving as a beacon to guide you back to the center. And don't worry about getting lost, Oban is small enough that a wrong turn only leads to a new discovery.

Getting Your Bearings: Maps and Applications

To truly embrace Oban like a local, you'll need certain tools to navigate its streets, trails, and more. Whether you prefer paper maps or digital maps, we have the finest ways to navigate.

Paper Maps: Your first trip should be the Visitor Information Centre, which offers a free Oban town map. It emphasizes major roadways, attractions, and parking lots, as well as a convenient harbor inset. These maps are basic, yet ideal for rapid reference. Local booksellers like Waterstones on George Street sell more comprehensive Ordnance Survey maps (such as the OS Explorer 376). These are ideal for hiking or day visits to destinations such as Kerrera and Loch Etive.

Smartphone Applications:

Google Maps: A credible resource for walking routes, food places, and public transportation. It works well in Oban's town center, although service may be poor in outlying regions. Download an offline map of Oban before you come in case the Wi-Fi is spotty.

Maps.me: This software is really useful for offline navigation. It has trails and smaller streets that are ideal for exploration outside the core. Load the Oban area into your hotel's Wi-Fi, and you're all set.

The VisitScotland app provides tailored guides, event listings, and attraction information for Oban. It's more useful for organizing your day on the fly than for navigating.

CalMac Ferries App: If you're going island-hopping, this app provides real-time ferry schedules and ticket buying. Essential for journeys to Mull and Iona.

Local Signage: Oban has good signage, particularly around the harbor and key attractions. Look for brown visitor signs pointing to attractions such as McCaig's Tower and the distillery. Walking trails, such as the walk to Ganavan Sands, are clearly marked, but longer excursions require a map.

Wi-Fi and Connectivity: Free Wi-Fi is accessible in cafés such as The Pokey Hat on George Street and the Visitor Information Centre. If you're not from the UK, think about getting a local SIM card (Vodafone or EE) for data, Oban's 4G is reliable in town but weaker in rural locations. The Visitor Information Centre can direct you to SIM dealers.

Tips for Using Maps and Apps: Download apps and offline maps ahead of time to conserve data. Mark your accommodation and important sites using a pen on a paper map for easy reference. When navigating, mix apps and landmarks, use Google Maps to select a restaurant, then seek for the North Pier sign to confirm your location. If you're hiking, use apps like Maps.me for trails, as Google might be inaccurate off-road.

Pro Tip: Ask locals for directions; they sometimes know shortcuts or picturesque routes that apps miss. For example, if you ask a pub bartender for the shortest way to McCaig's Tower, you may receive a gratuity for a quieter route. And don't worry about getting lost; Oban is small, and every turn is a photo opportunity.

Wrapping Up

There you have it, your guide to arriving in Oban and hitting the ground like a seasoned adventurer! You're ready to make Oban your own, from wandering around the busy town center to picking up maps at the Visitor Information Centre, identifying landmarks like McCaig's Tower, and navigating using apps. What's first on your list: getting a coffee by the harbor or pursuing the perfect view? Let's keep the journey going!

Chapter 4

TRANSPORTATION WITHIN OBAN.

Now, you have gotten to Oban, and it's time to figure out how to get about this charming Scottish town and its stunning environs. Oban has transportation alternatives for everyone, whether you want to explore the harbor, take a ferry to a nearby island, or cruise to a magnificent lookout. From wandering on foot to hiring a car, this chapter is your go-to resource for getting around like a local effortlessly and cheerfully. Let's look at the best ways to explore Oban and beyond!

WALKING: EXPLORING OBAN BY FOOT

Let's start with the most effective approach to soak in Oban's magic: walking. This town is designed for strolling, with a compact center, colorful streets, and views that will have you stopping every few meters to take photos. Trust me, your feet are soon to become your preferred form of transportation.

Why Walk? Oban's town center is a walker's paradise, with everything from the harbor to McCaig's Tower within a 15-minute stroll. You'll pass seafood shacks, eccentric stores, and quaint bars while taking in the fresh sea air. Walking is free, environmentally beneficial, and allows you to discover hidden gems such as a street performer or the ideal sunset viewpoint. Plus, it's the ideal way to experience Oban's laid-back culture.

Key Routes: Kick things off at the harbor, where the ferry station and North Pier pulse with life. Stroll along George Street to shop and dine, and while you're there, stop at the Oban Chocolate Company for a treat. Head up Stafford Street to the Oban Distillery, which is only a 5-minute stroll from the dock. Corran Esplanade north to St. Columba's Cathedral offers a picturesque walk with the water shining alongside you. Feeling energized? The 10-minute uphill trek to McCaig's Tower provides breathtaking views of the town and islands, well worth the calf exercise.

Insider Tips:

- Wear comfortable, durable shoes, the cobblestones near the harbor can be uneven, and the uphill approaches are steep.
- Explore early or late for a more relaxed atmosphere since summer crowds may bottleneck George Street.
- For longer hikes, always bring a light jacket and a water bottle.
- When navigating to sites such as the War and Peace Museum, landmarks such as the distillery might help you keep on track.
- Stop at the North Pier's "Oban" sign for a quick selfie; it's worth it!

Walking is the heart and soul of visiting Oban, allowing you to soak up every detail at your own leisure. You'll feel like a native in no time.

Local Bus Routes and Schedules

Local busses are a cost-effective and convenient option for trips outside of the town center or to surrounding locations. Oban's bus network, operated by West Coast Motors, connects the town to suburbs, beaches, and even farther afield, making it convenient to explore without a car.

Main Routes: The Service 405 is your go-to for local loops, with stops at Ganavan Sands (10 minutes, £2) for a beachy retreat and Atlantis Leisure for family fun. Service 1 travels to Dunbeg and Connel (15-20 minutes, £3), which is ideal if you are staying near outside town. For longer trips, the Service 918 goes to Fort William (1.5 hours, £10), passing by Loch Linnhe's breathtaking sights. Buses begin in Argyll Square or the bus station near the train station, both in the heart of Oban.

Schedules and Fares: Buses operate every 30-60 minutes from 7 a.m. to 6 p.m., however service is reduced in the evening and on Sundays. Single tickets in Oban start at £1.50 and can be paid with exact cash or a contactless card. If you're hopping on and off frequently, a day pass (£6-£8) is an excellent value. Check schedules at westcoastmotors.co.uk or get a timetable at the Visitor Information Centre on North Pier.

Insider Tips:

Arrive a few minutes early; buses are timely. Ask the driver to confirm your stop, especially at Ganavan Sands, where the drop-off is a short walk from the shore.

If you're going to Fort William, reserve online in the summer to ensure a spot. The buses are clean and comfortable, but carry a food for longer trips. When coming to a rural stop, wave to alert the motorist. This is small Scottish town, so anticipate a pleasant atmosphere!

Taxis and Rideshares: Getting Around Easily

Need a fast ride or to transport hefty bags? Taxis are the solution in Oban, providing a simple method to get around, particularly for short trips or late evenings.

Traditional taxis rule the roost since ride-sharing applications like Uber do not exist here.

Finding Taxis: Look for taxi stands at Argyll Square, the rail station, or the ferry port. Local taxi firms such as Oban Taxis (01631 564666) and A&B Taxis (01631 567777) are dependable and efficient. You can call to reserve or flag one down in busy areas, although pre-booking is recommended for early ferries or high season.

Fares and Uses: A ride within the town (for example, from the harbor to the distillery) costs between £5 and £11. Outlying locations such as Ganavan Sands and Dunbeg cost between £10 and £20 to visit. Fares are metered, however please clarify pricing for longer travels. Taxis are ideal for traveling to mountainous destinations like McCaig's Tower without hiking, or for returning from a pub after a few whiskies.

Insider Tips: Save a cab number on your phone; hailing on the street is uncommon. Drivers are friendly and full of local knowledge, so ask them about their favorite sites. Splitting a taxi is a cost-effective option for groups. Request a wheelchair-accessible car when booking. Taxis are more expensive than buses, yet they are invaluable when it comes to speed and convenience.

Bike Rentals for Eco-Friendly Exploration

Ready to cycle your way through Oban? Cycling's a fun, green way to explore the town and adjacent environs, helping you cover more land than walking while enjoying the fresh air. Oban is hilly, however there are flat routes suitable for casual bikers.

Where To Rent: Oban Cycles on George Street is the go-to destination for hybrid cycles and e-bikes, which cost between £15 and £30 per day. E-bikes are ideal for handling hills or longer trips, especially if you aren't a professional rider. Rentals include helmets, locks, and route ideas. In July and August, motorcycles sell quickly, so book ahead of time.

Best Routes: The Ganavan Sands trail (2 miles from the town) offers a flat, picturesque ride along the shore that is perfect for novices or families. For a little extra adventure, take the ferry to Kerrera and pedal its peaceful lanes, ideal for a picnic. The Oban to Connel route (6 miles) is a cycling path that runs beside the A85 and offers views of Loch Etive. Stick to indicated trails since some highways lack dedicated bike lanes.

Check your brakes and tires before you head out hills can be severe. Pack a raincoat and food, and secure your bike during pauses. Helmets are required, and ask the rental store for a repair kit for extended trips. If riding isn't your thing, stick with e-bikes or flat routes like Ganavan. The coastal wind and views make every pedal worthwhile!

Ferries to Nearby Islands: Schedules and Tips

Oban is known as the "Gateway to the Isles," and ferries transport visitors to adjacent islands such as Mull, Lismore, and beyond. CalMac Ferries operates these services, which are dependable and picturesque, making island hopping a highlight of your trip.

Key Routes: The Oban-Craignure (Mull) ferry is the most popular, with links to Tobermory and Iona. The Oban-Lismore ferry provides a calmer option for hiking or cycling. For a lengthier expedition, choose Colonsay (2.5 hours, £15). Ferries run 3–6 times every day, with more frequent trips in the summer. Check calmac.co.uk for schedules, since tides and weather might change things.

Insider Tips: Purchase tickets online or at the ferry station, but book early for summer or car spots. When traveling as a foot passenger, you'll have more freedom to move around. However, be mindful of peak season crowds and plan accordingly. Don't forget to pack a jacket for the deck, as it can get windy - but it's a great spot for dolphin-watching. Grab a snack at the terminal's cafe before your trip and stay updated on the weather to minimize delays. The ferry is wheelchair accessible via ramps; contact CalMac in advance for specific details.

CAR RENTALS FOR NAVIGATING THE REGION

Renting a car is a great option for maximum independence, especially for day trips to Glencoe or Kilmartin. Oban's car hire choices are limited but trustworthy, offering you the freedom to explore at your leisure.

Where To Rent: Enterprise and Hertz operate near the rail station, with small cars starting at £40 per day. Book online to get better prices, and make your reservations early in the summer. You must have a valid driver's license (international permits are acceptable) and be at least 21 years old. Smaller cars are ideal for narrow Highland routes.

Driving Tips: While Oban's roads are tolerable, rural routes can be windy. Park at Longsdale Car Park (£5 per day) or book accommodation that includes parking. Use a GPS or Maps.me for navigating because rural signage is scarce. Fuel up at Tesco on Lochavullin Drive; stations are few outside of town. Ganavan Sands (10 minutes), Glencoe (1 hour), and Kilmartin Glen (45 minutes) are all excellent historical destinations.

Tips: Compare costs on Kayak and look into drop-off fees if returning elsewhere. Manual cars are less expensive than automatics. If you're staying in Oban, you might not need a car because walking and ferries cover most bases.

Accessibility Options for Travelers

Oban is making itself more hospitable to all tourists by providing accessible transportation options. The town center's flat walkways are wheelchair-friendly, while certain harbor sections have cobblestones; stick to George Street for better pathways. West Coast Motors buses feature low floors and ramps; contact drivers for help. Taxis have wheelchair-accessible cars; reserve with Oban Taxis and clarify your needs. Ferries include ramps and accessible cabins; contact CalMac for further information. Oban Cycles can recommend flat routes and e-bikes for simpler cycling. The Visitor Information Centre provides accessible information and can suggest step-free attractions such as the distillery. Always call beforehand to confirm lodging or tour accessibility.

Wrapping Up

This is your guide to zipping around Oban! Whether you're wandering the harbor, biking to Ganavan, or taking the ferry to Mull, you're ready to explore comfortably. What's your next step: grab a bike or catch a ferry sunset? Let's keep the journey going!

Chapter 5

ACCOMMODATION IN OBAN.

You've your heart set on Oban, and now it's time to choose the ideal spot to stay after a day of exploring harbors, sipping whiskey, or island-hopping. Oban has a bed to suit every taste and budget, whether you want a posh resort, a cozy guesthouse, or something completely unique like glamping under the stars. This chapter is your guide to navigating the town's accommodation landscape, from upscale to budget-friendly, with tips on how to find the best deals and make your stay memorable. Let's have a look at your Oban vacation house!

Overview of Accommodation Options.

Oban's accommodation options are as diverse as its scenery, with something for everyone, including solo travelers, families, romantics, and budget backpackers. As a small costal town, most places are within walking distance of the harbor and major sights such as McCaig's

Tower, so you're never far from the excitement. Here's a brief overview of what's on offer.

You'll find luxurious resorts with spa vibes and coastal views, ideal for a splurge. Budget-friendly hotels keep things basic and economical, making them suitable for individuals who want to spend their money on ferries rather than luxury accommodations. Boutique guesthouses exude warmth, frequently featuring home-cooked meals and personalized touches. For something unique, consider glamping pods or historic cottages, which bring adventure to your doorstep. The majority of options are concentrated in the town Centre (George Street, Corran Esplanade) or immediately beyond, with a few spreads along the coast for added views.

Prices vary by season; plan to pay £100-£300 per night for luxury, £50-£100 for budget hotels, and £60-£150 for guesthouses during peak summer (June-August). Off-season (November-March) rates are often lower, sometimes by 20-30%. Many accommodations offer breakfast and have Wi-Fi, while parking might be difficult in the center. Oban got you covered, whether you want a luxury suite or a unique pod. Let's explore your options!

Luxury Resorts.

If you're in the mood to spoil yourself, Oban's finest resorts provide pampering with a view of the Highlands. These spots prioritize comfort, excellent service, and the "I'm on vacation" vibe, making them ideal for couples or anybody looking for a memorable stay.

What To Expect: Imagine luxurious accommodations with soft bedding, on-site restaurants selling fresh seafood, and amenities such as spas or hot tubs. Many resorts along the coast, providing panoramic views of the Firth of Lorn and adjacent islands. Summer prices often range from £150 to £300 per night, with breakfast generally included.

Top Picks:

The Perle Oban hotel (Corran Esplanade): This waterfront treasure combines contemporary comfort and Victorian charm. The rooms have sea views, rainfall showers, and cozy robes. The restaurant is well-known for its local scallops, and the bar has an excellent whiskey collection. Rates start at £180 per night. Early booking is recommended for harbor-facing accommodations.

Knipoch Hotel (6 miles south on the A816): This is a rural home getaway with groomed gardens and loch views. Think fireplaces, four-poster beds, and a dining room with venison and oysters. It's pricey (£200-£300 per night), but ideal for a romantic getaway. Free parking is a benefit.

Why Choose Luxury? These resorts are great for recuperating after a day of adventure or commemorating a particular occasion. They prioritize luxury above budget think spa treatments or a bottle of wine with a sunset view. Families may find them less practical, but couples or lone travelers seeking comfort may like the atmosphere.

Insider Tips: Book 3-6 months in advance for summer, since premium places fill up quickly. Ask about packages that include spa treatments or ferry tickets to save money. Check to see whether parking is included, since some resorts in town charge extra.

Budget-Friendly Hotels

Are you watching your wallet? Oban's budget-friendly hotels provide clean, comfortable lodgings at reasonable prices, allowing you to spend more money on fish and chips or ferry journeys. These are ideal for families, lone travelers, or anybody in need of a cozy bed.

What To Expect: Simple rooms featuring comfy mattresses, en-suite bathrooms, Wi-Fi, and, in many cases, a full breakfast. Many are conveniently positioned, just steps from George Street or the harbor. Summer rates vary from £50 to £100 per night, while winter rates range from £40 to £70.

Top Picks:

Muthu Alexandra Hotel (Corran Esplanade): This no-frills riverfront hotel has comfortable rooms and sea views. Breakfast is a complete Scottish variety, and the ferry station is just a 5-minute walk away. Rates start at £60 per night. Perfect for families and groups.

Lancaster Hotel (Esplanade): Simple yet cheery, with affordable rooms and a bar for a post-adventure pint. It's a little antiquated, but the location and pricing are outstanding (£50-£80 per night). Request a room that faces the sea.

Why Choose Budget? These hotels are all about value, clean, convenient, and central, freeing up funds for adventures like a Mull Day trip. They're less showy but dependable, with friendly personnel that know Oban inside and out.

Insider Tips: Book early during the summer because affordable slots fill up quickly. Look for deals on Booking.com or straight from hotel websites. Check to see whether breakfast is included; it will save you money. Parking might be limited, so please confirm availability.

Boutique Guesthouses.

Boutique guesthouses are ideal for experiencing Oban's charm. These small, sometimes family-run establishments are like staying with a buddy who knows all the best local secrets. Ideal for couples or solo visitors seeking a personalized experience.

What To Expect: Consider cozy rooms with unique design, homemade breakfasts (typically served with local vegetables), and hosts who give tips over tea. Many are housed in ancient structures, which give charm. Rates range from £60 to £150 per night, with breakfast generally included. The locations vary; some are central, while others are a short walk from town.

Top Picks:

Glenbervie Guest House (Dalriach Road): A Victorian jewel near McCaig's Tower with chic rooms and an excellent breakfast (try the smoked salmon). The hosts are quite welcoming. Rates start at £80 per night. A 10-minute stroll to the harbor.

Greystones B&B (Breadalbane Street): A boutique charmer with sea views and stylish design. The brunch is a highlight, with homemade pastries and local eggs. Rates range from £100 to £140 per night. Perfect for romantics.

Why Choose a Guesthouse? These stays are intimate, with 4-10 rooms, so you can expect personalized service. They're great for travelers who prefer character than cookie-cutter motels. Families may require larger accommodations, so check availability.

Insider Tip: Book directly with guesthouses to get potential discounts or benefits such as complimentary upgrades. Inquire about dietary requirements, most cater to vegan or gluten-free diets. Parking is often free but limited, so secure a place.

Unique Stays (e.g., glamping, historic cottages).

Want something out of the ordinary? Oban's unique accommodations, such as glamping pods and antique cottages, offer a sense of adventure to your journey. These are ideal for vacationers seeking an unforgettable experience.

What To Expect: Options include renovated cottages with stone walls and glamping pods with coastal views. Some are rustic, while others are contemporary, but each has a unique vibe. Rates range greatly (from £60 to £200 per night), and sites are frequently outside of the city core for added peace & quiet.

Top Picks:

Oban Glamping (near Ganavan Sands): Cozy pods with beds, heating, and communal amenities are within a 10-minute drive from town. Wake up to views of the sea and gaze at the stars at night. Rates: £60-£100 per night. Perfect for couples or lone explorers.

Barriemore Cottage (Connel, 5 miles north): A historic stone cottage with a contemporary interior, fireplace, and garden. Sleeps 4-6 people, ideal for families or parties. Rates: £120-£180 per night. Car recommended.

Why Choose Unique? These vacations are all about the experience, whether it's toasting marshmallows at a glamping site or cozying up in a cottage. They're less handy for rapid town access yet unrivaled for atmosphere.

Insider Tip: Book early because unique stays are limited. Check the amenities, some glamping locations have communal bathrooms. Bring clothes for chilly nights, especially in spring and autumn. If you're going out of town, confirm your transportation options.

Most Recommended Accommodation

Can't decide? Here's a selection of our top recommendations across categories, based on location, value, and visitor feedback.

Luxury: The Perle Oban Hotel; Waterfront elegance ideal for couples.

Budget: Muthu Alexandra Hotel; Central, family-friendly, and excellent value.

Boutique: Greystones B&B Chic and cozy, perfect for romance.

Unique: Oban Glamping (Ganavan Sands) offers scenic pods for travelers.

These accommodations strike a mix between location, comfort, and Oban's charm, assuring a memorable visit. Check availability early, particularly for the summer.

Selecting the Suitable Accommodation for You

With so many options, how do you choose? It's all about tailoring your stay to your travel preferences. This is a brief guide:

Solo Travelers: Glenbervie and other budget hotels or guesthouses provide affordable lodging and a communal atmosphere. Centralized locations save time.

Couples: Luxury resorts (The Perle) or boutique guesthouses (Greystones) provide a romantic atmosphere. Book a sea-view room.

Families: Muthu Alexandra, a budget hotel, has family rooms; for more space, consider a cabin. Check for child-friendly amenities.

Inexpensive Travelers: To save money, stay in inexpensive hotels or go glamping. For better deals, book during the off-season.

Adventure Seekers: Glamping or cottages near trails are ideal for outdoor enthusiasts. Make sure you have access to a car for day excursions.

Returning Visitors: To shake things up, try a different guesthouse or a unique stay.

Consider the location (central for convenience, seaside for views), amenities (breakfast, parking, Wi-Fi), and your budget. If you're island hopping, choose a location near the ferry station. Use Chapter 8's itinerary to ensure that your stay corresponds to your goals.

Bookkeeping Tips and Tricks

Ready to book your stay? Here's how to get the greatest deals while avoiding pitfalls:

Book Early: Summer reservations should be made at least 3-6 months in advance, particularly for luxury or unique accommodations. Winter appointments can be made at the last minute to get better pricing.

Compare Platforms: Find deals on Booking.com, Expedia, and hotel websites. Direct reservations may offer bonuses such as complimentary breakfast.

Look for Packages: Some resorts include ferry tickets and meal credits. Inquire about midweek or off-season savings.

Read Previews: For guest feedback, use TripAdvisor or Google, but make sure you read current reviews to ensure accuracy.

Confirm Details: Check the parking, cancellation policies, and breakfast inclusions. Ask about early check-in if you're arriving by boat.

Use Local Resources: The Visitor Information Centre can assist with last-minute reservations and recommendations.

Avoid Peak Pitfalls: July and August, as well as festival weeks (such as the Oban Games), are in high demand. Have a backup plan ready.

Pro Tip: Sign up for hotel newsletters or follow Oban tourism on social media for exclusive deals. In this bustling town, a little planning goes a long way.

Wrapping Up

Here you have it your guide to selecting the ideal Oban accommodation! From opulent resorts to eccentric glamping, you're in for a cozy, unforgettable stay. What's your style a sea-view suite or a rustic cottage? Let's continue planning your Oban adventure!

Chapter 6

TOP TOURIST ATTRACTIONS.

Oban may be small, but it's packed with exciting attractions and experiences. With its stunning viewpoints, historic castles, renowned whisky, and nearby island getaways, there's something for everyone to discover. Get ready to explore this charming coastal town and capture its beauty through your camera lens. Let's dive in and uncover the best of Oban!

McCaig's Tower: Stunning Views of Oban

First up is Oban's skyline icon, McCaig's Tower. Perched on Battery Hill, this Colosseum-inspired edifice is the town's most renowned sight, and believe me, it's worth the hype. Local banker John Stuart McCaig built it in 1897 as a memorial to his family (and a job-creation project), but it's more of a circular stone folly with epic vistas than a tower.

What's The Draw? The 10-minute uphill trek from George Street is strenuous, but once there, you'll be rewarded with panoramic views of Oban's harbor, the Isle of Mull, and the distant Hebrides. It's a photographer's dream, particularly around sunset when the sky becomes pink. The tower's arches and gardens are ideal for picnics or simply taking in the landscape.

Insider Tips: Wear strong shoes, since the path can be steep and slippery after rain. Avoid the summer throngs by visiting early or late. The tower is open every day and free to enter, but wear a jacket because it is windy up there. Locals enjoy taking nighttime strolls, so if you're lucky, you could see a bagpiper practicing. Don't miss this one; it's Oban's postcard moment.

Oban Distillery: A Taste of Scottish Whisky.

If you visit Scotland, you must sample the whisky, and Oban Distillery is the best site to do so. Tucked in the heart of town on Stafford Street, this 1794 jewel is one of Scotland's oldest operational distilleries, producing mellow, peaty single malts that whisky enthusiasts like.

What's The Draw? The distillery provides hour-long tours (£15-£20) that take visitors behind the scenes, past shining copper stills, oak barrels, and the delicious aroma of malted barley. You'll learn how Oban's 14-year-old whisky obtains its smokey, sea-salty flavor, and you'll get to sample a little dram (or two) at the conclusion. The gift shop is loaded with whisky-themed items that make ideal mementos. It's a cozy, private encounter, rather than a touristic mega-tour.

Insider Tips: Book tours online at obanwhisky.com, especially during the summer, when groups are small (max. 16). Tours run every day, but check the schedule; morning hours are calmer. Tastings need an 18-year-old minimum, however children over the age of eight are welcome to join the tour. To keep the warm fuzzies going, visit a neighboring pub for lunch. This is a must-see for whisky enthusiasts or anybody interested in Scotland's liquid gold.

Dunollie Castle: History & Heritage

Dunollie Castle, a rocky 13th-century fortification located just a 15-minute walk north of Oban's city, takes you back in time. Perched on a rock with views of the harbor, this castle-turned-museum, home to the MacDougall clan for generations, is a treasure mine of Scottish history.

What's The Draw? The castle remains are fascinating, with decaying stone walls and a tower house to explore. The neighboring Dunollie Museum (£8 entrance) delves into the MacDougall family history, featuring exhibits like as clan weaponry, ancient pictures, and even a 17th-century clothing. The surroundings are lovely, with wooded walks and a weaving shed where you could see a live demonstration. It's an ideal combination of history and landscape, suitable for people of all ages.

Insider Tips:

Wear comfortable shoes; the journey from town is level but may be muddy. Open from April to October, 10 a.m. to 4 p.m.; visit dunollie.org for activities such as storytelling days. Pack a picnic to enjoy in the gardens. The castle is not entirely accessible (steep steps), so contact ahead if you require mobility assistance. History buffs and families will enjoy this look into Oban's history.

Oban War and Peace Museum's Local Stories

For a dose of local heart and spirit, visit the Oban War and Peace Museum on Corran Esplanade. This small, volunteer-run museum portrays the town's history via two perspectives: its role in war time (particularly WWII) and its peaceful communal spirit.

What's The Draw? The museum, which is free to enter (donations are encouraged), is crammed with odd displays such as vintage uniforms, wartime letters, and fishing boat models. You'll discover how Oban's harbor operated as a WWII naval station and hear stories about local heroes. The "peace" side focuses on Oban's fishing tradition and communal life, with nostalgic images and recollections from locals. It's a fast visit (30-60 minutes), but surprisingly moving, with volunteers that like chatting.

Insider Tips: Open every day in the summer, with shorter hours in the winter, visit obanmuseum.org.uk. It is completely accessible, with ramps and no steps. Combine it with a walk along the Esplanade to St. Columba's Cathedral. Bring a few pounds to give; it helps keep this hidden gem going. Ideal for history aficionados or those who enjoy a good narrative.

St. Columba's Cathedral: Architectural Gem.

Oban isn't only whisky and castles; it also has a spiritual aspect. St. Columba's Cathedral, a stunning Gothic structure on Corran Esplanade, is the seat of the Roman Catholic Diocese of Argyll and the Isles. Its spire rises above the shoreline, giving it a prominent landmark.

What's The Draw? This cathedral, built in 1959, combines modern and traditional design elements, including elaborate stained-glass windows and a tranquil interior. The altar, fashioned from Italian marble, is a standout, and the sea views from the windows are nearly exquisite. It's a calm place to ponder or appreciate the building, and it's free to visit. If you prefer a more in-depth experience, look for occasional organ recitals or services.

Insider Tips: Open every day; dress appropriately (no shorts or headgear). It's a 10-minute walk from the harbor and completely accessible via ramps. Visit in the morning for beautiful lighting through the glass. Photographers and architecture enthusiasts will like it, but it also provides a peaceful respite from the hustle and bustle of city life.

Atlantis Leisure: Family-Friendly Entertainment

Are you traveling with kids or just looking for some active fun? Atlantis Leisure on Dalriach Road is Oban's go-to destination for family-friendly entertainment. This community center is helpful on rainy days or when you need a break from touring.

What's The Draw? Atlantis has a swimming pool with a flume, a soft play area for children, and a gym for adults. In addition, there is a sports center for badminton and climbing, as well as outdoor tennis courts. The prices are modest (£5-£10 per activity), and the cafe is ideal for food. It's a 10-minute walk from the town and has a friendly, local atmosphere.

Insider Tips: Check atlantisleisure.co.uk for schedules; pool hours change. Book activities over the summer to prevent disappointment. Bring towels and change for the lockers. Families will appreciate it, but solitary travelers or couples may enjoy the gym or courts too. Pair with a visit to neighboring Ganavan Sands for a great day out.

GANAVAN SANDS: SCENIC BEACH WALK

Want some sand between your toes? Ganavan Sands, a sandy beach two miles north of Oban, is a popular destination for picturesque hikes and coastline views. It's the ideal place to unwind and see the raw beauty of Scotland's west coast.

What's The Draw? This crescent-shaped beach features golden sand, calm surf, and views of Mull and Lismore. The coastal path from Oban (40-minute walk or 10-minute bus ride) is level and picturesque, passing through grassy dunes. If you're feeling courageous, go swimming (it's frigid!), picnic on the beach, or go shell hunting with the kids. The sunsets here are very spectacular.

Insider Tips: Take the Service 405 bus from Argyll Square (£2), or walk down Corran Esplanade. There is free parking available if you are driving. Layer up since the winds might be gusty. The beach is accessed by a ramp to the sand. Visit early to avoid summer crowds. This serene retreat will appeal to nature enthusiasts and families alike.

Pulpit Hill, Panoramic Lookout Point

Hike to Pulpit Hill; A picturesque lookout just south of Oban, for an absolutely breathtaking views. It's less touristic than McCaig's Tower but as breathtaking, with panoramic views without the crowds.

What's The Draw? The 20-minute walk from the city (by Ardconnel Road) leads to a grassy hilltop with views of Oban's harbor, Kerrera, and distant mountains. It's an ideal location for photographs, a peaceful time, or a picnic. Locals use it for dog walks, so you'll feel as if you're in on a secret.

Insider Tips: Wear sturdy shoes since the trails might be muddy. Visit around daybreak for golden light, or noon for great vistas. Visit is free, however there are no amenities, so bring your own water. Uneven ground prevents complete access. Hikers and photographers will like this off-the-beaten-path treasure.

Oban Phoenix Cinema - Cultural Entertainment

Oban Phoenix Cinema on George Street is a great place to have some culture or a treat on a wet day. This independent, volunteer-run theater is a popular neighborhood gathering place, presenting everything from blockbusters to indie films.

What's The Draw? The intimate 150-seat cinema has a nostalgic ambiance, with reasonably priced tickets (£8-£10) and a snack bar serving popcorn and local ice cream. Look for unique events, such as live-streamed theater or vintage cinema evenings. It's a 5-minute walk from the harbor, ideal for an evening out.

Insider Tips: Reserve tickets at obanphoenix.com, particularly for new releases. Open every day, including family matinees. Hearing loops make it fully accessible. Combine with supper on George Street for a fantastic evening. Moviegoers and families will appreciate this glimpse into rural life.

Kerrera Island: Day Trip Adventure.

Are you ready for an island escape? Kerrera Island, a 15-minute boat journey from Oban, is a little experience that feels far away. This small, craggy island is ideal for a day trip packed with history, hiking, and relaxation.

What's The Draw? Kerrera has it all: the ruins of Gylen Castle from the 13th century, coastal trails where you can spot seals, and quiet beaches. The Kerrera Tea Garden offers homemade scones, and the island's car-free atmosphere is pure bliss. Ferries (£3 return) run hourly during the summer. Pack a picnic and hike the 4-mile loop to get the full experience.

Insider Tips: Book ferry tickets at kerrera-ferry.co.uk for foot passengers only. The trails are uneven, so wear hiking boots. Open all year, but the weather is best during the summer. Rough terrain prevents full access. This island getaway is ideal for adventurers and families alike.

Wrapping Up

There you have it: Oban's top ten attractions, ready to make your vacation unforgettable! What's first on your list, between the vistas from McCaig's Tower and the natural beauty of Kerrera? Let's keep the Oban adventure going!

CHAPTER 7
DINING AT OBAN

Welcome to Oban, where the dining scene is as dynamic as the waterfront views. Referred to as the "Seafood Capital of Scotland," this seaside jewel delivers dishes that will make your taste buds dance, from fresh-off-the-boat scallops to substantial Scottish staples. Oban has something to suit every taste, whether you want a formal supper, a quick café lunch, or vegan cuisine. With tips on where to eat, what to try, and how to dine like a local, this chapter is your guide to the town's gastronomic wonders. Grab a napkin and prepare to dive in!

Seafood Specialties: Fresh from the Harbor.

Oban's nickname is not just for show; its harbor is a seafood lover's dream, with boats delivering the freshest catches every day. If you enjoy oysters, prawns, or fish so fresh that it virtually swims to your plate, you're in for a treat.

What To Expect: Menus feature local favorites such as plump West Coast scallops, delicious Langoustine prawns, and creamy Cullen skink (smoked haddock chowder). From upscale restaurants to harborside shacks, seafood can be found everywhere. Prices range from £10 to £15 for casual dishes to £20-£30 for gourmet platters. Spots near North Pier and George Street serve as the harbor's hub.

Top Spots:

Oban Seafood Hut (North Pier): A green shack near the ferry port serves famed fish & chips, lobster rolls, and oyster platters for £8-£18. Eat while standing or perched on a nearby seat with a view of the water. Cash only, open daily throughout the summer.

Ee-Usk (North Pier): This is a beachfront restaurant with panoramic windows and a cuisine of seared scallops, grilled fish, and seafood platters (£15-30). Make reservations for dinner, it's a local favorite.

Tips: Early arrival is recommended for the freshest catches, especially at informal spots like the Seafood Hut, which can sell out quickly. Ask servers about the day's specials, which are frequently the finest choices. To complete the experience, pair your meal with a local brew or dram of Oban whiskey. If you're new to seafood, consider a mixed plate to get a taste of everything.

Traditional Scottish Cuisine.

Beyond seafood, Oban's dining scene highlights Scotland's hearty staples. Consider dishes that will warm you up after a windy beach stroll, served in snug pubs or traditional restaurants.

What To Expect: Steak and ale pie, cranachan (a dessert of cream, raspberries, and oats), and haggis (spiced minced beef, sometimes served with neeps and tatties, turnips and potatoes) are staples. These dishes are rich, cozy, and ideal for taking up Oban's vibe. Main courses at pubs often cost £10-£20, with slightly higher prices in more premium spots.

Top Spots:

The Lorne Bar (on Stevenson Street): A vibrant pub with a delicious haggis plate and venison pie (£12–£18). The atmosphere is purely Scottish, with live music on select nights. Walk-ins are welcome.

Cuan Mor (George Street): A brewery serving upscale pub cuisine, such as haggis-stuffed chicken or smoked salmon with oatcakes (£14-£22). Perfect for families and groups.

Insider Tips: Haggis is surprisingly palatable, especially when served with a whiskey sauce. Look for lunch specials at pubs to save a few pounds. If you're coming on Burns Night (January), look for special meals that celebrate Scottish cuisine. For added flare, pair with a locally brewed craft beer from Cuan Mor's brewery.

International Dining Options.

Looking for something more that Scotland has to offer? Oban offers a startling selection of different tastes, from

Italian to Indian, to bring diversity to your dining experiences.

What To Expect: Italian pastas, spicy Indian curries, and even Chinese takeaways are largely concentrated around George Street and Argyll Square. With main courses ranging between £10 and £20, these spots are informal. They are ideal for a change of pace or if your party has diverse interests.

Top Spots:

Piazza (North Pier): An Italian restaurant with harbor views that serves wood-fired pizzas and silky seafood linguine (£12–£20). The tiramisu is a must. Book a summer supper.

Taj Mahal (George Street): A charming Indian restaurant with tasty curries ranging from butter chicken to vegetable korma (£10–£18). If you're exhausted from a day excursion, this is an excellent takeout option.

Insider Tips: International spots like Piazza can get crowded on weekends, so make reservations ahead of time. Ask about spice levels in Indian restaurants; they are ready to modify. If you have finicky eaters, these meals provide both familiar and local dishes. To complete the experience, pair with a glass of wine or a mango lassi.

Cafes and Bakeries for Quick Bite

Need a coffee or a quick bite between attractions? Oban's cafés and bakeries are ideal for enjoying a croissant, a sandwich, or a relaxing time with a view.

What To Expect: Expect cute, independent cafés offering locally roasted coffee, homemade scones, and light meals such as soups and sandwiches. Prices range from £3 to £10, and several spots are located on George Street or near the port. Ideal for breakfast or a mid-afternoon pick-me-up.

Top Spots:

The Pokey Hat (George Street): This is a quirky cafe that serves delicious coffee, fresh scones, and vegan-friendly sandwiches (£4-8). The free Wi-Fi and harbor views make it an ideal work-from-Oban location.

Food from Argyll (Argyll Square): A deli-café serving local cheeses, oatcakes, and substantial soups (£5-10). Pack a picnic for Ganavan Sands. Open every day.

Insider Tips: Get to cafes early for the tastiest pastries scones go fast! Look for daily deals, which are commonly displayed on chalkboards. Many have takeaway options, ideal for boat journeys or treks. If you're looking for a sweet treat, try a tablet (a Scottish fudge-like confection) at The Pokey Hat.

BEST RESTAURANTS AND HIDDEN GEMS

Are you looking for the best? Here's a handpicked selection of Oban's top restaurants and under-the-radar spots, organized by taste, mood, and local love:

Ee-Usk (North Pier, £15-£30): Here is ideal for seafood with a view; try the scallop starter and grilled hake. Book your window seats early.

Cuan Mor (George Street, £14-£22): Excellent tavern for Scottish dishes and artisan beer. The outside terrace is a summertime highlight.

Baab (Corran Esplanade, £15-£25): A hidden treasure serving Middle Eastern-inspired dishes like as lamb kofta with local touches. Quiet and comfortable, ideal for couples.

The Olive Garden (Railway Pier, £12-£20): A lesser-known Italian restaurant with seafood spaghetti and harbor views. Perfect for lunchtime specials.

Insider Tips: Make reservations at popular spots like Ee-Usk, especially during the summer or at festivals. Hidden treasures like Baab welcome walk-ins but are busier on weekends. Ask the servers for wine or whiskey pairings; they know their stuff. These establishments represent Oban's diversity, from excellent dining to intimate corners.

Dietary Considerations: Vegan, Gluten-Free, And More

Oban's dining scene is surprisingly diverse, including options for vegan, gluten-free, and other dietary preferences. You won't have to eat plain salads here!

What's Available? Most restaurants serve vegetarian and vegan dishes, such as veggie curries at Taj Mahal and plant-based burgers at Cuan Mor. Gluten-free choices are prevalent, particularly in seafood (grilled fish) and soups. Cafés like The Pokey Hat offers vegan pastries and gluten-free scones. Prices are similar to ordinary menus, with specialist items costing £1-£2 extra.

Top Spots:

Cuan Mor: Serves vegan haggis and gluten-free pies, with clear menu marks.

The Pokey Hat: A go-to for vegan wraps and gluten-free pastries. Inquire about daily promotions.

Piazza: Gluten-free pizza bases and vegan cheese are available; contact ahead to check.

Tips: Check menus online or call ahead to confirm dietary options, particularly at smaller spots. The Visitor Information Centre may recommend restaurants that are allergy-friendly. If you're vegan, ask eateries about plant-based milk options, such as oat or soy. Oban's cooks are accommodating, so don't hesitate to request changes.

Dining Etiquette and Tipping

Dining in Oban is casual, but a few local customs can help you fit in. Scots are hospitable, and Oban's restaurants reflect this warm friendliness.

Etiquette: Dress casual; jeans and a sweater are acceptable, even at more upscale spots like Ee-Usk. Arrive on time for bookings; if you are late, a brief call will suffice. Table service is usual in restaurants and pubs, while informal cafés and seafood shacks need orders to be placed at a counter. Be nice to the staff—Scots appreciate "please" and "thank you." If you're in a pub, don't flash money to get served; simply wait your turn at the bar.

Tipping: Tipping is optional but appreciated for good service. If a service fee is not charged, leave 10-15% in restaurants. For informal spots such as cafés or the Seafood Hut, round up the amount or leave £1-2. Use cash for tiny tips because card machines may not offer a tip option. If you're impressed by a meal (say, at Baab), a larger tip demonstrates your appreciation.

Insider Tips: If you're confused about etiquette observe the natives; they're laid-back and welcoming. Clear your table fast in congested spots to free up space. If you're dining during a festival (such as the Seafood Festival), anticipate slower service and hefty tips for hardworking employees.

Wrapping Up

There you have your guide to Oban's wonderful dining scene! From harbor-fresh seafood to quaint cafés and hidden gems, you're in for a gourmet journey. What's first on your list: scallops or haggis? Let us keep this Oban adventure delightful!

Chapter 8

OUTDOOR ACTIVITIES AND ADVENTURES.

Hello, adventure seeker! Oban is beckoning, and it's ready to offer a playground of outdoor fun that will have your pulse racing and your camera clicking. This village, located on Scotland's craggy west coast, is surrounded by spectacular hills, dazzling waterways, and an abundance of wildlife. Oban got you covered whether you want to hike to a panoramic vantage point, kayak through calm lochs, or glimpse a dolphin in the wild. This chapter is your guide to the best outdoor activities and adventures, from trails to tours, all wrapped in the unmistakable Highland spirit. Grab your hiking boots and let's explore the wild side of Oban!

HIKING TRAILS AROUND OBAN.

Oban's hills and coastal walks are a hiker's delight, with trails for all skill levels, from easy strolls to strenuous climbs. With views of islands, lochs, and mountains, you'll be pausing for pictures as well as refreshments.

Top Trails:

Pulpit Hill (1-2 hours; easy): This pleasant 2-mile round-trip ascent begins on Ardconnel Road just south of town and goes to a grassy overlook with panoramic views of Oban's port and Kerrera Island. Ideal for beginners or a sunset hike. Free, but no facilities, so bring your own water.

Beinn Lora (3-4 hours; moderate): A 5-mile trek near Benderloch (15-minute drive north) leads through the forest to a 620-foot top. You will view Loch Etive and the Glencoe highlands. Park in the Beinn Lora car park; the trails are well-marked but can be muddy.

Kerrera Island Loop (3-5 hours; moderate): Take the 15-minute boat to Kerrera (£3 return) and then hike a 4-mile circle via Gylen Castle ruins and coastal bluffs. It's a combination of grassy walkways and rocky coasts, with opportunities to observe seals. Start early to catch the first ferry.

Why Hike? Oban's trails combine coastal beauty with Highland drama, and they're easily accessible from town. You'll experience the fresh air, see wildlife like deer and eagles, and earn your fish and chips afterwards. Most trails are free, and the views are invaluable.

Insider Tips: Wear strong, waterproof footwear; trails get slick after rain. Pack clothes, a raincoat, and snacks; the weather can change quickly. Check trail conditions at walkhighlands.co.uk and get an Ordnance Survey map (Explorer 376) from Waterstones for comprehensive itineraries. To avoid private territory, stay on marked pathways and inform someone of your plans for longer excursions. Solo hikers, families, and groups will all enjoy this walk.

Water Activities: Kayaking, Sailing, and More

Oban is surrounded by water, the Firth of Lorn, Loch Etive, and other lochs so it's not surprising that water sports are popular here. Whether you're an experienced paddler or a beginner, the water is your playground.

What's on Offer?

Kayaking: Paddle along the Oban shoreline or to Kerrera for calm waters and seal sightings. Sea Kayak Oban provides half-day tours (£60-£80) from Ganavan Sands, which include gear and guides. Beginners are welcome; no prior experience required.

Sailing: Take a sailing tour to explore the islands or learn the ropes. Oban Sailing Club offers basic courses (£50-£100) over the summer, or you may arrange a private boat charter (£200+/day) for a more luxurious experience.

Stand-up paddleboarding (SUP): Try SUP for a fun, core-burning adventure. Wild Diamond Watersports in Ganavan rents boards (£15 per hour) and provides lessons (£40).

Why Try It? Water activities allow you to experience Oban from a different perspective, imagine skimming by cliffs or spotting otters up close. The waters are often tranquil, especially during the summer months, and guided tours make it accessible to people of all ages.

Insider Tips: In the summer, book with outfits like Sea Kayak Oban (seakayakoban.com) at least a week in advance. Splashes happen, so wear quick-dry clothing and pack a change. Strong winds might cause trips to be canceled, so check the weather forecast. Most operators supply wetsuits, but bring sunscreen on sunny days. Ideal for couples, families, and single explorers seeking a splashy excitement.

Wildlife Watching: Seals, Birds, and Dolphins.

Oban's waterfront and marine life is spectacular, with seals, seagulls, and even dolphins stealing the show. Whether you're a binocular-toting birder or simply enjoy animals, wildlife watching here is enchanting.

What To See:

Seals: Common and grey seals relax on Kerrera's beaches or appear near Oban's port. Look for them on kayak trips or ferry voyages to Mull.

Birds: Look for puffins, guillemots, and sea eagles on the islands. Staffa Tours (staffatours.com) provides boat trips to Staffa (£40-£60), a puffin hotspot, from May to July.

Dolphins And Whales: Bottlenose dolphins and minke whales frequent the Firth of Lorn. Sea Life Adventures (sealife-adventures.co.uk) offers wildlife cruises from Clachan Seil (20-minute drive, £70-£100) with professional guides.

Why Should I Watch? Oban's waterways and islands are alive with life, and you don't have to be an expert to appreciate them. Guided tours provide context, but even a boat trip might result in sightings. It's a relaxing approach to connect with nature.

Insider Tips: Book wildlife tours 2-3 weeks in advance, particularly for Staffa or whale viewing. Bring binoculars, a camera with a zoom lens, and thick clothing, boats get cold. Morning trips have calmer seas and more active creatures. Check the tide periods for coastal walks to see seals. This spectacular experience will delight families, couples, and lone travelers alike.

Fishing trips and charters.

Want to throw a line in Scotland's waters? Oban's fishing trips are an excellent chance to test your luck, whether you're looking for mackerel, cod, or simply the excitement of the water.

What's Available? Half-day fishing cruises (£50-£80) leave Oban's port for inshore seas to catch mackerel or pollack. Oban Sea Fishing (obanseafishing.co.uk) provides beginner-friendly trips with poles and bait provided. Full-day trips (£150-£250) take dedicated anglers to deeper areas in search of haddock and ling. Some trips let you to retain your catch, which is ideal for a DIY seafood supper.

Why Fish? It's a hands-on approach to learn about Oban's maritime history while also enjoying spectacular coastline vistas. It's fun for beginners or experts since guides provide tips and stories. Ideal for parties or families seeking a shared adventure.

Insider Tips: In the summer, book charters a month in advance with companies such as Oban Sea Fishing. Wear waterproof clothes and nonslip shoes; boats will supply life jackets. Check the weather forecast; severe waves might cause trips to be cancelled. Ask about preparing your catch; some places will prepare it for you. Morning trips are ideal for calm water and aggressive fish.

Golfing In Scenic Surroundings

Golfers, prepare to swing in style, Oban's courses feature tough holes with Highland backgrounds that make every shot seem spectacular. Even if you're not a pro, the landscape is well worth the green fees.

Top Courses:

Glencruitten Golf Club (one mile from town): An 18-hole, par-62 course set in a forested valley. Known as "Oban's hidden gem," it has challenging fairways and vistas of Ben Cruachan. Green fees range from £30 to £40 per day. Club rentals are available (£15).

Taynuilt Golf Club (10 miles east): A 9-hole course with loch and mountain vistas, ideal for a relaxing round. Fees £20-£25. Less crowded, ideal for beginners.

Why Golf? Oban's courses combine sport and environment, providing a calm respite from tourist hotspots. They're cheaper than Scotland's well-known courses, and the locals are kind.

Insider Tips: Tee times may be booked at glencruittengolfclub.co.uk or by calling Taynuilt (01866 822268). Summer mornings are the busiest; escape crowds by going in the afternoons. Wear golf shoes and bring a raincoat; the weather might change. Bring your own clubs if feasible, as rental options are limited. Solo players, couples, and groups will all appreciate the relaxed atmosphere.

GUIDED TOURS FOR OUTDOOR ENTHUSIASTS

If you want an expert to lead the way, Oban's guided tours are an excellent way to explore the outdoors. From hiking to wildlife, these tours provide expertise and simplicity to your journey.

Top Tours:

West Coast Tours (westcoasttours.co.uk) provides day trips to Mull, Iona, or Staffa that include wildlife viewing and guided walks. Boats sail from Oban's harbor, where guides tell island history while seeing seals and puffins.

Oban Walking Tours (obanwalkingtours.co.uk): Offers coastal tours to Ganavan Sands or Pulpit Hill (£20-

£40), with guides describing the area flora and history. 2-4 hours; appropriate for all fitness levels.

Sea Life Adventures (sealife-adventures.co.uk): Provides wildlife and photography tours from Clachan Seil, with a concentration on whales, dolphins, and eagles (£80-£120). Small groups and skilled guides.

Why Take a Tour? Guides bring Oban's landscapes to life with stories and observations, and they also manage logistics such as ferry tickets and trail navigation. Ideal for first-timers, families, or anybody looking for a more in-depth experience without having to prepare ahead.

Insider Tips: Book tours 2-4 weeks in advance, particularly during the summer, through operator websites or the Visitor Information Centre. Wear sturdy shoes and layers; most tours are conducted rain or shine. Inquire about group sizes; smaller tours (8-12 people) are more intimate. Check to see whether meals or gear are included; some offer snacks or binoculars. Photographers, nature enthusiasts, and curious tourists will like these.

Wrapping Up

There you have it, Oban's outdoor experiences, ready to fill your journey with excitement and scenery! What's first on your list, whether it's ascending Pulpit Hill, kayaking to Kerrera, or playing golf at Glencruitten? Let us continue this crazy Oban voyage!

Chapter 9

CULTURAL EXPERIENCES

Hey, culture vulture! Oban is more than just stunning views and seafood; it has a bustling cultural scene that will transport you to the heart of Scottish life. This coastal jewel is bursting with opportunities to interact with its heritage and culture, from foot-tapping ceilidhs to eccentric art stores and Gaelic traditions. This chapter is your introduction to Oban's cultural gems, whether you're a music fan, a history enthusiast, or simply interested in the local vibe. Grab a coffee and let's explore the heart of this Highland town!

Local Music and Ceilidhs.

If you want to experience Oban's heartbeat, look for live music or attend a ceilidh (pronounced "kay-lee"), a traditional Scottish dance gathering that emphasizes fun and community. Music is woven into Oban's fabric, and you're in for a surprise.

What's the Vibe? Bagpipes, fiddles, and accordions are expected to fill taverns with upbeat music. Ceilidhs are vibrant gatherings when locals and guests dance to reels and jigs, frequently with a caller directing them through the steps, no expertise is required! Regular music evenings are held at venues such as The Lorne Bar (Stevenson Street) and Cuan Mor (George Street), with either free entry or a nominal cover charge (£5-£10). Ceilidhs are held at events such as the Oban Games (August) or in community halls such as the Corran Halls.

Why Try It? It's pure joy; imagine spinning, laughing, and perhaps a small dram of scotch. You will meet locals, make new friends, and feel as if you are in a Scottish film. Even if you are shy, simply seeing the excitement is contagious.

Insider Tips: Check whatsonoban.com for music schedules, as evenings vary. Ceilidhs are casual, so dress comfortably. Arrive early to get a seat or participate in a dancing class (which is often given prior to performances). If you're in a bar, get a pint of local ale to drink between songs. Suitable for couples, solitary travelers, and families with older children.

Art Gallery and Craft Shops

Oban's creative energy is evident in its art galleries and craft shops, where you can peruse local works and purchase unique souvenirs. These locations offer a glimpse into the town's creative essence, inspired by its coastal beauty.

What To Expect: Small galleries display paintings, pottery, and textiles created by Argyll artisans. Craft stores sell handcrafted jewelry, tartan scarves, and unique presents. Most are located on George Street or near the port, with prices ranging from £10 for trinkets to £100 or more for unique art.

Top Spots:

The Jetty Gallery (George Street): This is a cozy gallery showcasing bright seascapes, ceramics, and glasswork by local artists. Prices range from £200 to £500. Open daily and ideal for browsing.

Oban Craft Shop (Stafford Street): Stocked with Celtic-inspired jewelry, crocheted wraps, and whiskey barrel crafts. Ideal for gifting. It is convenient to visit the distillery because it is nearby.

Why Should You Visit? You'll view Oban's landscapes through the eyes of an artist while also supporting small businesses. It's a low-key way to enjoy the culture, whether you're buying or just browsing. Ideal for people of all ages, particularly those who cherish unique findings.

Insider Tips: Talk to store owners; they often share anecdotes about the artists. Look for labels that say "made in Scotland" to prove authenticity. Avoid the weekend throngs by visiting on weekdays. If you're sending art home, inquire about packaging; most stores are experts. Combine with a coffee from The Pokey Hat nearby for the ideal morning.

Historic Walking Tours

Want to learn about Oban's heritage? Historical walking tours are an excellent opportunity to explore the town's history, from clan conflicts to the busy harbor days. These guided strolls bring history to life from a local's viewpoint.

What's On Offer? Tours often visit sights like as McCaig's Tower, Dunollie Castle, and the Oban Distillery while blending in stories about the MacDougall clan and WWII naval history. Oban Walking Tours (obanwalkingtours.co.uk) provides 1–2-hour hikes (£15-£25) that begin in Argyll Square. Private trips for families or groups cost between £50 and £80. Some focus on specialized topics, such as Victorian Oban or maritime heritage.

Why Do It? You'll experience Oban via a historical perspective, led by knowledgeable experts who know every nook and corner. It's entertaining for all ages, and you'll learn interesting stuff to impress your trip companions. Walking is also an excellent way to get to know the town.

Tips: Book trips online or at the Visitor Information Centre, particularly during the summer. Wear comfortable shoes and a raincoat; tours run rain or shine. Morning trips are calmer, while afternoon tours provide excellent lighting for photographs. Inquire with guides about secret areas, such as historic smuggling routes. History aficionados and interested tourists will enjoy this in-depth look.

Gaelic Culture and Language Fundamentals

Oban's Gaelic origins are rich, and exploring this ancient culture is a unique opportunity to connect with the

Highlands. From music to language, Gaelic (pronounced "Gallic") enriches your vacation.

What's the Deal? Scotland's indigenous language, Gaelic, is still spoken in Argyll. You'll hear it in songs at ceilidhs or see it on bilingual signage (e.g., "Oban" means "An t-Òban" in Gaelic). Some institutions, such as Dunollie Museum, features Gaelic storytelling or weaving demonstrations (£8 entry). The Corran Halls occasionally offer Gaelic music nights and seminars, particularly during events like as the Oban Winter Festival (November). For a fast introduction, the Visitor Information Centre offers complimentary Gaelic phrase leaflets.

Basic Phrases to Try:

Halò: Hello.

Tapadh leat: Thank you.

Slàinte: cheers/health

Why Explore It? Learning a few phrases or hearing Gaelic music is like entering Scotland's soul. It's a polite reference to local tradition and a pleasant way to interact with locals, who like it when visitors try it.

Insider Tips: Before a ceilidh, practice phrases from the appendix's "Useful Local Phrases"; these are excellent icebreakers. Check dunollie.org for Gaelic activities, as schedules vary. If you want to learn more, contact the Visitor Information Centre about short courses (which are sometimes available in the summer). Perfect for cultural aficionados or anybody looking for a more in-depth Oban experience.

VISITING LOCAL MARKETS AND FAIRS.

Oban's markets and fairs are a fun chance to meet people, buy handcrafted items, and sample regional cuisines. These activities take place all year and highlight the town's communal spirit.

What To Expect: The Oban Farmers' Market (Argyll Square, first Saturday of each month) sells local cheeses, smoked salmon, and baked items for £2 to £10. Summer festivals, such as the Oban Seafood Festival (September), include food vendors, live music, and crafts. Smaller markets at the Rockfield Centre sell art and knitwear. Expect a cheerful atmosphere, with merchants eager to speak.

Why Should You Visit? Markets provide a taste of Oban's local life, with fresh scones, tartan scarves, and banter with stallholders. They're inexpensive and ideal for souvenirs or picnic provisions in Ganavan Sands.

Insider Tips: Check whatsonoban.com for market dates. Bring cash (small sums) for booths that don't accept cards. Arrive early to have the finest variety, particularly for seafood and pastries. If you're visiting a fair, hang around for live music or children's entertainment. Families, couples, and lone travelers will love the vibrant atmosphere.

ENGAGING IN COMMUNITY EVENTS

Oban's community gatherings are where the town's benevolence shows the most. Participating in events such as Highland games and winter festivals makes you feel like a part of the family.

Key Events:

Oban Games (August): A Highland festival with pipers, dancers, and athletes tossing cabers. Tickets cost £10-£18 and are available at Mossfield Park. Expect crowds, so book your accommodations early.

Oban Winter Festival (November): Christmas markets, light displays, and ceilidhs illuminate the town. Most events are free to attend, with mulled wine and crafts for sale at vendors.

Burns Night (January): Pubs such as The Lorne hold suppers with haggis, poetry, and whiskey toasts (£20-£40). A comfortable way to honor the poet Robert Burns.

Why Should You Join? These festivities are pure Oban filled with humor, tradition, and local pride. You'll interact with locals, experience new foods, and create memories that will outlive any souvenir. Perfect for people of all ages, especially those who enjoy immersive experiences.

Insider Tip: Look for event dates on visitscotland.com or local posters. Book tickets for ticketed events such as the Oban Games at least a month in advance. Dress for the weather, as outdoor activities might be chilly. Arrive early to secure good seats, and don't be timid about joining dances or conversations locals encourage newcomers. If you're traveling alone, events are an excellent way to meet people.

Wrapping Up

Oban's cultural experiences enrich your journey with music, art, and community spirit! What's first on your list when you're dancing at a ceilidh, exploring The Jetty Gallery, or saying "Slàinte" at a Burns Supper? Let's

Chapter 10

SOUVENIRS AND SHOPPING: BRINGING OBAN HOME

Oban is a treasure mine of souvenirs and unique gifts that will keep the Highland charm alive long after you've returned home. From cozy tartan scarves to smokey whiskey and creamy fudge, this coastal jewel caters to every taste and budget. Whether you're browsing George Street's shops or looking for local crafts, this chapter is your introduction to Oban's shopping scene. Let's take a look at the best spots to bring home a bit of Scotland!

Independent Shops and Boutiques

Oban's local shops and boutiques are at the core of its retail appeal, giving unique articles and customized service that you won't get in a chain store. Whether it's a trinket or a statement piece, these spots are ideal for acquiring something unique.

What's The Vibe? Imagine cozy, family-run boutiques stocked with anything from Celtic jewelry to nautical-themed furnishings. Most are clustered between George Street and Stafford Street, making them convenient to visit in one day. The prices range from £5 for little presents to more than £50 for high-quality items. The proprietors frequently offer tales about their products, lending a human touch.

Top Picks:

The Oban Gift Shop on George Street: A one-stop store for postcards, magnets, and Scottish-themed mugs (£3 to £20). Perfect for inexpensive souvenirs or last-minute gifts. Open every day.

Seasalt Cornwall (George Street): A store selling coastal-inspired clothes and accessories, such as striped scarves and raincoats (£20-£80). Ideal for a stylish remembrance.

Why Shop Here? These shops embody Oban's personality, imagine sea-inspired items and friendly service. You're supporting local companies, and the diversity ensures there's something for everyone, from children to grandparents.

Insider Tips: Ask merchants for recommendations; they may guide you to hidden gems. Bring cash for smaller shops, as some may not accept credit cards. Avoid the weekend crowds by visiting during the week. For a relaxing break, combine your shopping with a coffee at The Pokey Hat nearby. If you don't have much time, head to George Street, which is the shopping district.

Scottish Craft and Woollens

Nothing says Scotland like handcrafted products and cozy woollens, and Oban's artisan shops provide both. Highland-inspired souvenirs include tartan blankets and exquisite ceramics. The shops specialize in Harris Tweed, tartan scarves, and knitted sweaters, as well as pottery and woodwork influenced by Oban's surroundings. Prices range from £10 for modest crafts (such as coasters) to more than £100 for superior woollens. Look for labels that say "Made in Scotland" to ensure authenticity. Most stores are located on George Street or near the waterfront.

Top Picks:

Oban Craft Shop, Stafford Street: A hidden gem stocked with tartan bags, hand-carved whiskey barrel coasters, and Argyll ceramics (£10-£60). The staff's understanding of local craftspeople is a plus.

The House of Tartan (North Pier): Specializes in clan-specific tartans, including kilts and scarves. They'll assist you locate your clan's pattern, which is ideal for heritage enthusiasts.

Why Should I Buy? These crafts are ageless, whether you're snuggling up in a wool scarf or giving a tartan souvenir. They're strong, meaningful, and shout "Scotland!" Excellent for all ages, especially if you value quality over quantity.

Insider Tips: Look for genuine Harris Tweed labels (handwoven in the Outer Hebrides). If you have a certain clan tartan in mind, inquire about bespoke orders. Bargaining is uncommon; however, some stores provide discounts on numerous goods. Pack woollens carefully to avoid moths on the trip home. Visit early in the day to have the finest variety.

Whiskey and Local Spirits Retailers

Oban's whiskey legacy is world-renowned, and its shops are a paradise for spirits enthusiasts. Whether you're a whiskey connoisseur or simply want a bottle to toast your vacation, you'll find enough to drink and savor.

What's Available? The standout is Oban Distillery's 14-year-old single malt, which has smokey, sea-salty flavors. You can also discover various Scottish whiskies, local gins, and artisan beers. Shops sell bottles ranging from 50ml minis to uncommon editions (£200+). Most are located near the distillery or waterfront.

Top Picks:

Oban Distillery Shop (Stafford Street): The place to go for Oban's own whiskey, as well as rare distillery-only bottles. They provide taste notes to assist you make your decision. Open every day and located only feet from George Street.

Whisky Vaults (George Street): A specialty shop with a large selection of malts, gins (including Isle of Kerrera Gin) and gift packages. The staff is knowledgeable, making it welcoming to newcomers.

Why Shop Here? A bottle of Oban whiskey is the ultimate souvenir, sippable history in a glass. Gins and beers add variety, and the shop's experience makes selection simple. Ideal for adults or gifts.

Insider Tips: After the tour, stop by the distillery shop to purchase unique bottles. If you don't have much packing room, ask about travel-sized minis. If you're traveling overseas, check the UK duty-free restrictions (1L per person). Purchase bubble wrap from stores for secure packaging. If you don't drink, try whisky-infused chocolates (£5-£10) instead.

Art Gallery and Studio

Oban's art sector is a love letter to its scenery, with galleries and studios displaying local artists. These spots are great for picking up a unique artwork or simply immersing yourself in creativity.

What To Expect: The galleries include paintings, prints, and sculptures inspired by the sea, islands, and Highlands. Prices range from £15 for postcards to more than £500 for genuine pieces. Smaller workshops sell cheap ceramics and jewelry. The majority are located on George Street or North Pier, with a few tucked away in more peaceful areas.

Top Picks:

The Jetty Gallery (George Street): This is a bright place featuring seascapes, glasswork, and ceramics by Argyll artists (£20–£500). The crew shares the artists' tales, making it more personal. Open every day.

Rockfield Centre (Stevenson Street): A community arts venue that features rotating exhibits and cheap prints (£15-£100). If you want to learn by doing, look into seminars.

Why Should You Visit? Art conveys Oban's beauty in ways that photographs cannot, and you are supporting local artists. It's a low-pressure approach to browse, whether you're looking to buy or simply be inspired. Perfect for couples, lone travelers, and everyone who appreciates beauty.

Insider Tips: Ask about the painters' backgrounds, many live nearby and are inspired by Oban's scenery. Look for autographed prints for low-cost art. Galleries frequently pack items for transport; clarify before purchasing. Visit throughout the week for a more relaxed atmosphere. Combine with a historical walking tour (Chapter 10) for a cultured day.

Food Souvenirs: Smoked Salmon, Cheese and Tablet

Oban's food souvenirs are a great way to take its delights home. These delicacies, which range from smokey salmon to crumbly cheeses and sweet tablets, are ideal for foodies or as gifts.

What to Find:

Smoked Salmon: Locally smoked, thick, and buttery, available vacuum-packed for transport (£10-£30 per 200g-500g). Try the Inverawe Smokehouses goods.

Cheese: Argyll cheeses, such as Isle of Mull Cheddar and Arran Blue, are creamy and assertive (£5-£15 per 200g). Look for handcrafted packages.

Tablet: A sweet, flaky, and buttery Scottish fudge that is sometimes flavored with whisky or vanilla (£3-£10 per 100g-300g).

Top Spots: Food from Argyll (Argyll Square): A deli offering smoked salmon, local cheeses, and tablet gift bundles (£5-£30). They will advise on travel safety choices. Open every day.

Oban Chocolate Company (George Street): Known for its tablet and whiskey truffles. Their gift boxes are ideal for sweet-toothed pals.

Why Should I Buy? Food souvenirs allow you to recreate Oban's flavors at home, imagine fish on bagels or tablet with tea. They're easy to pack and distribute, making them ideal for families or groups.

Insider Tips: Check vacuum-sealed salmon and cheese packaging for customs compliance (e.g., EU/USA limitations). Buy the tablet in small batches, it's expensive! Ask delis for taster samples to select your favorite. Keep food in your carry-on to minimize baggage disasters. Visit the Oban Farmers' Market (the first Saturday of each month) for new batches and specials.

Wrapping Up

Here you have it: your guide to Oban's shopping scene, complete with souvenirs to keep Scotland nearby! What's the first thing you think of when you grab a tartan scarf, a bottle of Oban whiskey, or a tablet? Let's keep the Oban adventure going!

Chapter 11

EXPLORING BEYOND OBAN: POPULAR DAY TRIPS

Hello, adventurer! Oban's harbor and whisky-soaked charm are only the beginning; explore beyond the town and you'll be treated to some of Scotland's most amazing day trips. From the vibrant alleys of Mull to the mystical shores of Iona and the ancient stones of Kilmartin Glen, these getaways are brimming with history, nature, and Highland magic. Whether you're taking a ferry to an island or traveling through rugged landscapes, this chapter will guide you through seven spectacular day trips that can all be completed in one day from Oban. We'll finish with tips for planning your ideal adventure, so grab your backpack and let's explore the delights just outside Oban's doorstep!

Isle of Mull: Tobermory and Duart Castle.

Let's start with the Isle of Mull, a bustling island located just a 50-minute ferry trip from Oban. Mull is a crowd-pleaser, combining beautiful villages, magnificent castles, and abundant wildlife.

Why Go? Tobermory, Mull's major hub, is a postcard-perfect town with a rainbow-painted waterfront. Stroll around the harbor, see the Mull Aquarium (perfect for kids), or get fish and chips at The Pier Café. For sweet souvenirs, visit quirky shops such as Tobermory Chocolate Shop. For history buffs, Duart Castle (£8 entrance, 20 minutes from Craignure) is a 13th-century MacLean clan castle with battlements, clan artifacts, and sea views. Mull is also a wildlife sanctuary, so keep a watch out for otters, sea eagles, and perhaps whales.

Getting There: Take the CalMac ferry from Oban to Craignure. From Craignure, take the Service 96 bus to Tobermory, or rent a car in Oban for more flexibility. Buses to Duart are infrequent, so a car or cab is recommended. Total travel time: 7-9 hours.

Insider Tips: In the summer, book ferry tickets at calmac.co.uk at least a week ahead. Take the 8 a.m. ferry to make the most of your day; try to return by 6 p.m. Mull's weather changes swiftly, so dress in layers. Pack a picnic or dine in Tobermory, as Duart's café is minimal. Mull's charming and adventurous atmosphere will appeal to families, couples, and lone visitors alike.

Isle of Iona: Abbey and Spiritual Significance.

If you want to find calm and a touch of the divine, the Isle of Iona is the place to go. This little island, a 10-minute ferry ride from Mull, is a spiritual retreat with pristine beaches and an ancient monastery that will astound you.

Why go? The main attraction is Iona Abbey, which was founded by St. Columba in 563 AD and is one of Scotland's holiest locations. Wander around its renovated cloisters, old crosses, and calm graveyard, taking in the spiritual atmosphere. Beyond the monastery, Iona's white sand beaches, like as Port Ban, provide turquoise seas and calm hikes. The island is car-free, with rolling hills and an unrivaled sense of tranquility. Stop by the Iona Craft Shop for handmade soaps, or get a scone at the St. Columba Hotel (£5-10).

Getting There: Take the Oban-Craignure ferry to Mull (£8), followed by a bus or cab to Fionnphort (1 hour, £10). The CalMac ferry to Iona takes 10 minutes (£4 roundtrip). Total trip time: 2-2.5 hours each way. West Coast Tours (£60-£80) provides guided Mull-Iona trips and handles all transportation.

Insider Tips: Iona is a popular destination, so book ferries and tours ahead of time. Wear sturdy shoes on abbey walks. Allow 5-7 hours to explore the abbey and seashore. Check the tide timings for beach access. Ideal for history buffs, spiritual seekers, or anybody seeking a quiet retreat.

Isle of Staffa: Fingal's Cave and Puffins (seasonal).

The Isle of Staffa is a must-see for anyone seeking a wild and almost bizarre experience. This uninhabited island, a one-hour boat ride from Oban, is known for its stunning geology and beautiful puffins, but it is only accessible from April to October owing to weather.

Why Go? Fingal's Cave, a sea cave with hexagonal basalt columns, is the highlight; its acoustics inspired Mendelssohn's Hebrides Overture. Walk the clifftop trail to peek into the cave and see puffins (May-July), seals, or dolphins. Staffa's raw, unadulterated beauty is remarkable, with little facilities and a focus on nature. Staffa Tours (£40-£60) provides 3-hour trips with one hour on the island.

Getting There: Book a boat tour from Oban's harbor with Staffa Tours or Turus Mara (staffatours.com). Daily departures in season, weather permitting. There are no public ferries; tours are the only way. Total travel time: 5-6 hours.

Insider Tips: Reserve tours 2-3 weeks in advance; cancellations are usual due to intense waves. Wear waterproof boots, the walkways are slippery. Bring binoculars to see puffins and a packed lunch (there is no food on Staffa). Morning trips have calmer seas. Ideal for wildlife enthusiasts, photographers, or families with kids over 5.

Island of Kerrera: Walking and History.

Want a short island getaway without the hassle? The Isle of Kerrera, a 15-minute ferry ride from Oban, is the way forward. It's small, tranquil, and full of history and trails, making it ideal for a half-day vacation.

Why Go? Kerrera's 4-mile circular walk takes you to Gylen Castle, a 16th-century ruin on a cliff with free entry and breathtaking views of Mull. Wander along calm beaches and meadows, keeping an eye out for seals and sheep. The Kerrera Tea Garden offers homemade cakes and is a comfortable visit. It's a hiker's heaven, devoid of cars and crowds. Allow three to four hours for the loop and tea break.

Getting There: The Kerrera ferry departs hourly at Gallanach, 2 miles south of Oban. There are solely foot passengers. See kerrera-ferry.co.uk for schedules.

Insider Tips: Book ferry tickets online for the summer. Wear hiking boots because the paths might get muddy. Pack water; the tea garden is a treat but not always open. Start with the 9 a.m. ferry to avoid crowds. Ideal for lone travelers, couples, and families seeking a low-key vacation.

Kilmartin Glen: Ancient Standing Stones and Cairns

History nerds, buckle up Kilmartin Glen, located 45 minutes south of Oban, is an archeological paradise with over 800 prehistoric structures, ranging from standing stones to ancient fortifications.

Why Go? Highlights include the Nether Largie Standing Stones, a 3,000-year-old alignment, and Dunadd Fort, a mountaintop where early Scottish monarchs were crowned. The Kilmartin Museum brings it all to life via artifacts and family-friendly exhibitions. To visit grave cairns, walk the linear cemetery route for 1-2 hours (free). The glen's uncanny beauty is a time machine. Lunch at Kilmartin Hotel completes the deal.

Getting There: Drive on the A816 or take the Service 423 bus from Argyll Square (1 hour). Buses are sparse; therefore, driving is preferable. Total travel time: 6-8 hours.

Insider Tips: Begin at the museum with a map and context. Wear sturdy shoes as the pathways are uneven. Open year-round; spring and fall are calmer. Allow time for 2-3 locations, including the museum. It's ideal for history aficionados or families with inquiring kids.

Inveraray, Castle and Jail

Are you craving a taste of Highland grandeur? Inveraray, a one-hour drive northeast of Oban, is a picture-perfect village on Loch Fyne with a magnificent castle and a peculiar jail.

Why Go? Inveraray Castle, home to the Duke of Argyll, is a fairy-tale picture of towers, magnificent apartments, and extensive gardens. The armory hall's musket display is iconic. Inveraray Jail is a living museum with actors portraying 19th-century convicts that is entertaining for all ages. Wander through the town's whitewashed streets and eat at The George Hotel. Allow two hours each attraction.

Getting There: Drive on the A85/A819 or take the Service 926 bus from Argyll Square (1.5 hours). Driving is ideal for flexibility. Total travel time: 7-9 hours.

Insider Tips: Book tickets online (inveraray-castle.com, inverarayjail.co.uk) to get the best deals. Open April through October; check winter hours. Wear comfortable shoes in the garden. Midweek trips avoid summer crowds. Perfect for families, couples, and history buffs.

Seil Island and the 'Bridge Over the Atlantic'

For a unique, offbeat adventure, visit Seil Island, located 20 minutes south of Oban and connected by the renowned Clachan Bridge, nicknamed the "Bridge Over the Atlantic" because to its stunning stretch across a tidal channel.

Why Go? The 18th-century bridge's humpback shape makes for a great photo opportunity. On Seil, go to Easdale, a historic slate mining community with a small museum. Hike coastal walks for views of Jura, or have seafood chowder at Tigh a Truish bar. Seil's calm charm is a refreshing respite. Allow 4 to 6 hours.

Getting There: Drive on the A816 or take the Service 418 bus to Clachan. There are bus stops near the bridge, and Easdale is only a short walk away. Driving is ideal for exploration.

Insider Tips: Open year-round; spring is best for calm hiking. Bring your camera for bridge views. Check the pub hours (tighantruish.co.uk). Layer up since coastal breezes can be severe. Ideal for couples or single visitors seeking a hidden gem.

Plan Your Day Trip

Are you ready to pick your escape? Here's how to plan the perfect day trip from Oban, whether you're looking for islands or history.

Pick Your Vibe: Mull for diversity, Iona for spirituality, Staffa for untamed environment, Kerrera for simplicity, Kilmartin for ancient history, Inveraray for grandeur, and Seil for peculiarities. Check Chapter 8 for combination itineraries (e.g., Mull and Iona).

Timing and Transportation: Trips last 4-9 hours, including travel. CalMac ferries (Mull, Iona, Kerrera) and Staffa Tours may be booked up to 1-2 weeks in advance at calmac.co.uk or staffatours.com. Enterprise rents vehicles for £40 per day to Kilmartin, Inveraray, and Seil. West Coast Motors buses (westcoastmotors.co.uk) are affordable, but verify schedules. Guided tours make island trips easier.

What To Bring: Bring a raincoat, sturdy shoes, drink, snacks, and a camera. Binoculars to see wildlife on Staffa or Mull. Check the weather, rain and wind can be troubling for ferries. Carry cash for small cafés and fees.

Insider Tips: Start early (8-9 a.m.) to maximize daylight. Book attractions online to get savings. Allow extra time for ferry delays. Eat at destination cafés or carry picnics for rural locations such as Staffa. Check whatsonoban.com for festival overlap. There's a vacation for everyone, solo, family, or couple.

Wrapping Up

This is your guide to seven great day trips from Oban! What draws you to Mull's colorful alleys or Staffa's wild caves? Let's keep the Highland adventure going!

Chapter 12

NIGHTLIFE AND ENTERTAINMENT

Hello, night owl! Oban's nightlife may not be as vibrant as Glasgow's, but this coastal jewel knows how to party after dark with cozy bars, toe-tapping music, and a true Scottish charm vibe. Oban has you covered, whether you want a pint in a historic tavern, a live fiddle session, or a calm waterfront stroll under the stars. This chapter is your guide to the town's nightlife, from busy places to seasonal events that will keep you entertained. Let's explore Oban's nightlife and make your evenings unforgettable!

Pubs & Bars: Where to Unwind

Oban's pubs and bars are the beating core of the city's nightlife, offering warm vibe, local beers, and lots of opportunities to meet with friendly locals. These areas are ideal for relaxing after a day of touring.

What's The Vibe? Expect cozy, historic pubs with crackling fireplaces, sophisticated bars serving craft beer, and everything in between. Most are on George Street or near the harbor and serve local beers, Oban whiskey, and hearty pub fare. The prices for a pint, cocktails, and drams are affordable. Many stay open until midnight or 1 a.m. throughout the summer.

Top Picks:

The Lorne Bar (on Stevenson Street): A historic tavern with a vibrant atmosphere, local brews such as Fyne brews, and plenty of whiskey. Try their haggis bites and hang around to chat with the regulars. Open daily.

Cuan Mor (George Street): A brewpub with its own specialty beers, a sea-view patio, and a burger and seafood menu. Ideal for parties or a relaxing dating night.

Insider Tips: Arrive before 8 p.m. to get a table, especially on weekends. Order at the bar; table service is not typical in pubs. Ask bartenders for whiskey recommendations; they are experts. Dress casually, with jeans and a sweatshirt. Visit bars throughout the week for a more relaxed vibe. Perfect for lone travelers, couples, or anybody looking for a cozy night.

Live Music Venues.

Oban's live music culture is fantastic, with pubs and venues featuring everything from traditional Scottish fiddles to modern acoustic concerts. If you enjoy decent music, you'll have a nice time.

What's On Offer? Expect to hear bagpipes, accordions, and ceilidh-style bands at traditional venues, as well as folk or indie artists in other locations. The Lorne Bar and The View (North Pier) offer free music evenings every week, with occasional cover charges for special events. The Corran Halls host larger concerts during festivals. Check whatsonoban.com for scheduling, as evenings vary.

Top Spots:

The Lorne Bar has regular sessions with local bands performing reels and jigs. Friday and Saturday evenings are the liveliest, with many dancers. Free entry, but bring a pint to support the vibe.

The View: A contemporary facility with sea views that hosts a variety of folk, rock, and ceilidh acts. Gigs are hit or miss, so keep an eye on their Facebook page for updates. Ticketed concerts cost between £5 and £8 to attend.

Insider Tips: Arrive early (7-8 p.m.) to get seats in tiny venues, which fill up quickly. Bring cash for cover charges and tip jars. Don't be afraid to join in on a ceilidh dance; locals will teach you the steps. If you're at Corran Halls, get your tickets online. Ideal for music fans or anybody seeking a taste of Scottish culture.

Theater and Cinema Experiences.

Oban's theater and cinemas offer cozy, community-driven entertainment. These locations are ideal for a relaxing evening, whether it's a movie or a live performance.

What's Available? The Oban Phoenix Cinema (George Street) is a 150-seat independent jewel that shows blockbusters, arthouse films, and live-streamed theater (£8-10). The Corran Halls stage plays, musicals, and comedies, particularly during festivals such as the Oban Winter Festival (tickets £10–£20). Both are conveniently located and have a pleasant local vibe.

Top Experiences:

Oban Phoenix Cinemas: Retro evenings feature current releases as well as classics such as Braveheart. The snack bar serves local ice cream. See obanphoenix.com for showtimes.

Corran Halls: Look for traveling Scottish plays or pantomimes in the winter. The location is small, with excellent acoustics. Book at corranchallenges.com.

Insider Tip: Buy movie tickets online to avoid lines; Corran Halls plays sell out during festivals, so book early. Both are accessible, including hearing loops. Combine a movie with supper at Cuan Mor for a great night out. Ideal for families, couples, and lone travelers looking for a relaxing evening.

Evening Harbor Walks.

Sometimes the best nightlife is beneath the stars, and Oban's port delivers with twilight walks that are both tranquil and breathtaking. It's the ideal way to end your day.

Why Walk? The harbor glows at night, with lights reflecting off the sea and McCaig's Tower illuminating the hill. Follow Corran Esplanade to St. Columba's Cathedral for a calmer vibe, or stroll along North Pier for views of ferries and fishing boats. The 1-2-mile courses are flat, free, and last 30-60 minutes, with benches for resting.

Highlights: Stop by the Oban sign on North Pier for a nighttime selfie. If you're lucky, you could spot a busker or a seal splashing about. The esplanade is peaceful, with views of Kerrera Island by moonlight. For a lengthier walk (40 minutes), go to Ganavan Sands, but carry a torch for safety.

Insider Tips: Wear a jacket; coastal winds are cool. Stick to illuminated routes around the bay or esplanade, and avoid unlit trails at night. Go after sunset (about 9 p.m. in summer) for the best glow. Pair with a pre-walk pint from The Lorne Bar. Ideal for couples, lone travelers, or anybody looking for a relaxing night.

Seasonal Nightlife Events.

Oban's nightlife receives a boost during seasonal events, when the town goes all out with festivals, markets, and parties. These are ideal occasions to get into the communal spirit.

Key Events:

Oban Games, August: This Highland games festival extends into the evening, with ceilidhs and bar sessions. Expect live music at The Lorne Bar or Corran Halls. Book your lodging ahead of time because pubs are always full.

The Oban Winter Festival (November): Features Christmas markets, light displays, and pop-up bars around the port. Argyll Square offers free admission, mulled wine, and live music. Check www.whatsonoban.com for scheduling.

Burns Night (January): Pubs such as Cuan Mor hold suppers with haggis, whiskey toasts, and poetry readings. A cozy and cultural night.

Why Should You Join? These events enhance Oban's nightlife with more music, cuisine, and festivities. You'll socialize with the locals, dance to bagpipes, and drink hot toddies under fairy lights. Perfect for people of all ages, particularly those who enjoy immersive experiences.

Insider Tip: Look for event dates on visitscotland.com or local posters. Book tickets for premium events such as Burns Night at least a month in advance. Dress warmly for outdoor festivals, layering is essential. Arrive early to secure a good place at markets or ceilidhs. These are ideal for solo travelers who want to meet new people.

Wrapping Up

Oban's nightlife and entertainment is ready to brighten your evenings! What are your plans for the night? Will you be drinking whiskey at The Lorne, dancing at a ceilidh, or strolling along the shimmering harbor? Let's keep the Oban adventure going!

Chapter 13

SUGGESTED ITINERARIES FOR MAKING THE MOST OF YOUR TIME

Hello, traveler! Planning your Oban adventure and unsure of how to include all the magic? We've got you covered with seven bespoke itineraries, whether you're looking for a fast weekend, a week of outdoor thrills, or a romantic getaway. These plans make use of Oban's charm, history, and untamed beauty, with seafood feasts, island hopping, and budget-friendly tips. Each itinerary combines must-see attractions, eating hotspots, and day excursions (Chapter 1 Trip), with tips tailored to your preferences. Grab a notebook and let's plan your ideal Oban trip!

Weekend Getaway (2-3 Days)

Ideal for: Busy people seeking a brief Highland break.

Overview: This 2-to-3-day plan explores Oban's attractions, combining town charm with a taste of the Isles.

Day 1: Oban Essentials

Morning: Arrive at Oban (by rail or car). Drop your baggage at the Muthu Alexandra Hotel. Stroll around the waterfront and have a coffee from The Pokey Hat. Visit Oban Distillery for a whiskey tour.

Afternoon: Lunch at Oban Seafood Hut (fish and chips). Climb McCaig's Tower for breathtaking views (free 15-minute walk). Explore the Oban War and Peace Museum (donations accepted).

Evening: Dinner at Cuan Mor (haggis-stuffed chicken). Relax with a pint at The Lorne Bar (live music).

Day 2: Island of Kerrera

Morning: Breakfast at Food from Argyll. Take the 9 a.m. Kerrera ferry. Hike the 4-mile circle to Gylen Castle (free for 3 hours). Snack at Kerrera Tea Garden.

Afternoon: Return by 2 p.m. Lunch at Piazza (pizza for £12). Visit St. Columba's Cathedral (free, 10-minute walk).

Evening: Dinner at Ee-Usk (scallops for £20). Evening harbor stroll around the North Pier (free). Optional: see a film at the Oban Phoenix Cinema.

Day 3 (Optional): Ganavan Sands.

Morning: Breakfast at the hotel. Ganavan Sands is a 40-minute walk or about £2 bus ride. Enjoy coastal views and a picnic. Depart by midday.

Insider Tip: Schedule boat and distillery visits at least a week in advance. Total cost: £150 to £200 per person (excluding transport to Oban). Pack comfortable shoes and a raincoat. Ideal for couples and friends.

Cultural Immersion (4-5 days)

Ideal for: Culture aficionados want to learn about Oban's heritage.

Overview: This 4-5-day itinerary focuses on music, history, and Gaelic traditions.

Day 1: Oban's Core.

Morning: Check into Glenbervie Guest House. Visit the Visitor Information Centre to get complimentary Gaelic phrase leaflets.

Afternoon: Lunch at The Pokey Hat. Tour of the Oban Distillery. Explore Dunollie Castle and Museum (15-minute walk).

Evening: Dinner at The Lorne Bar (venison pie, £14) with free live music. Check for ceilidh nights.

Day 2: Historical Walk

Morning: Breakfast at the guesthouse. Join an Oban Walking Tour (£20, 2 hours, Chapter 10) that explores McCaig's Tower and harbor history.

Afternoon: Lunch at Food from Argyll (soup £6). Visit the Oban War and Peace Museum (free). Explore The Jetty Gallery for local art (£20-£100).

Evening: Dinner at Baab (lamb kofta). Corran Halls hosts a play or concert in the evening (see the calendar).

Day 3: Island of Iona

Morning: Ferry to Mull and Iona with West Coast Tours, Visit Iona Abbey.

Afternoon: Picnic on Port Ban Beach (£5). Explore Iona Craft Shop.

Evening: Return by 6 p.m. Dinner at Cuan Mor (seafood plate for £22). Relax at The View (pint for £5).

Day 4: Local Culture

Morning: Start with a breakfast at the Pokey Hat (scone).

Visit the Rockfield Centre for free art exhibitions. Learn Gaelic phrases at the Dunollie Museum event (if available).

Afternoon: Lunch at Piazza (pasta for £12). Oban Craft Shop sells tartan presents ranging from £20 to £50.

Evening: Dinner at The Olive Garden (seafood linguine). Attend a ceilidh at The Lorne (free; check schedule).

Day 5 (Optional): Farmers' Market

Morning: Visit Oban Farmers' Market (first Saturday, Argyll Square). Depart by midday.

Insider Tip: 2 weeks in advance, plan your tours and Iona trip. Total cost: £300–£400 per person. Check whatsonoban.com for upcoming events. Ideal for lone travelers or groups.

Celsius. Outdoor Adventure (5-7 Days)

Ideal For: thrill enthusiasts who like hikes, kayaking, and wildlife.

Overview: With trails and island experiences, this 5–7-day plan explores Oban's untamed side.

Day 1: Oban Introduction.

Morning: Stay at Oban Glamping. Hike Pulpit Hill (free, 2-hour).

Afternoon: Lunch at Oban Seafood Hut. Kayak with Sea Kayak Oban (£60 for 3 hours).

Evening: Dinner at Cuan Mor (burger). Evening harbor stroll (free).

Day 2: Isle of Kerrera

Morning: go to the Isle of Kerrera by ferry. Hike to Gylen Castle (3 hours; free).

Afternoon: Tea at Kerrera Tea Garden. Return by 2 p.m. Lunch at The Poky Hat costs.

Evening: Dinner at Ee-Usk (cod, £20). A pint at The Lorne Bar costs.

Day 3: Isle of Staffa Morning

Morning: Staffa Tours boat trip. See Fingal's Cave and the puffins (seasonal).

Afternoon: Picnic on Board (£5). Return by 3 p.m. Visit Ganavan Sands (bus £2).

Evening: Dinner at Piazza (pizza for £12). Relax at The View (music for £5).

Day 4: Beinn Lora.

Morning: Drive to Beinn Lora (15 minutes). Hike the 5-mile path (3 hours, free).

Afternoon: Lunch at Benderloch Cafe. Visit St. Columba's Cathedral (free).

Evening: Dinner at Baab (kofta, £18). Cinema at Oban Phoenix.

Day 5: Wildlife Cruise.

Morning: Take a Sea Life Adventures dolphin and eagle tour from Clachan Seil.

Afternoon: Lunch at Tigh a Truish. Explore the Seil Island trails (free).

Evening: Dinner at The Olive Garden. Harbor stroll (free).

Days 6-7 (Optional): Mull

Day 6: Ferry to Mull. Visit Tobermory and Duart Castle. Return by 6 p.m.

Day 7: Hike McCaig's Tower (free). Depart.

Insider Tips: Book tours 2–3 weeks ahead. Total cost: £400–£600 per person. Pack hiking boots and waterproofs. Ideal for active couples and groups.

FAMILY-FRIENDLY TRIP (4 DAYS)

Ideal for: Families with children of various ages.

Overview: This 4-day plan blends family-friendly activities with Oban's attractions.

Day 1: Oban Fun

Morning: Stay at Muthu Alexandra Hotel. Visit Oban Chocolate Company.

Afternoon: Lunch at Oban Seafood Hut. Play at Atlantis Leisure (pool).

Evening: Dinner at Piazza (pizza). Harbor stroll (free).

Day 2 - Ganavan Sands

Morning: Bus to Ganavan Sands. Build sandcastles and picnic.

Afternoon: Lunch at Food from Argyll. Visit the Oban War and Peace Museum (free).

Evening: Dinner at Cuan Mor (children's menu). Cinema at Oban Phoenix.

Day 3: Isle of Mull.

Morning: Ferry to Mull. Explore Tobermory and Mull Aquarium.

Afternoon: Picnic in Tobermory. Return by 4 p.m. Visit St. Columba's Cathedral (free).

Evening: Dinner at The Lorne Bar (pie). It's early night.

Day 4: visit Dunollie Castle

Morning: Visit Children-friendly Museum and trails.

Afternoon: Lunch at The Pokey Hat (£8). Depart.

Insider Tip: Make your boat and Atlantis reservations at least one week in advance. Total cost: £200–£300 per person. Pack snacks and beach toys. Great for families with children aged 3 and above.

Budget Travel (3-4 days)

Ideal for: Budget-conscious travelers.

Overview: This 3-4-day plan takes use of Oban's free and low-cost jewels.

Day 1: Oban Freebies.

Morning: Stay at Oban Glamping. Visit McCaig's Tower (free).

Afternoon: Picnic at the harbor. Explore the Oban War and Peace Museum (free).

Evening: Dinner at Oban Seafood Hut. A pint at The Lorne Bar.

Day 2: Kerera

Morning: Ferry to Kerrera (£3). Hike to Gylen Castle (free).

Afternoon: Picnic on Kerrera (£5). Return by 2 p.m. Lunch at Food from Argyll costs £6.

Evening: Dinner at The Pokey Hat (wrap, £8). Harbor stroll (free).

Day 3: Ganavan Sands

Morning: Bus to Ganavan Sands. Beach stroll with picnic.

Afternoon: Go to St. Columba's Cathedral (free). Shop at Oban Craft Shop (£10-20).

Evening: Dinner at Taj Mahal (curry, £12). It's early night.

Day 4 (Optional): Farmers' Market

Morning: Visit the Oban Farmers' Market (£5-£10). Depart.

Insider Tips: Make sure to book your glamping trip early. Total cost: £100-£150 each person. Save money by taking public transportation or walking. Ideal for students and budget travelers.

FLEXIBLE SOLO TRAVELER'S GUIDE

Ideal for: Solo explorers with 3-5 days.

Overview: This customizable plan combines culture, nature, and social vibes.

Day 1: Oban Base

Morning: Stay at Glenbervie Guest House. Visit the Oban Distillery.

Afternoon: Lunch at Oban Seafood Hut. Hike Pulpit Hill (free).

Evening: Dinner at The Lorne Bar (pie), with free live music.

Day 2: Social Scene.

Morning: Join the Oban Walking Tour (£20). Coffee at The Pokey Hat.

Afternoon: Lunch at Food from Argyll. Visit Dunollie Castle.

Evening: Dinner at Cuan Mor. Attend a ceilidh at The View.

Day 3: Kerrera or Staffa.

Morning: Choose between Kerrera (ferry £3, walk free) and Staffa (tour £50, seasonal).

Afternoon: Picnic. Return by 3 p.m. Visit the Jetty Gallery (from £20 to £100).

Evening: Dinner at Baab. Harbor stroll (free).

Day 4-5 (Optional): Mull or Iona

Day 4: Ferry to Mull from Tobermory (aquarium). Return by 6 p.m.

Day 5: Iona Tour. Depart.

Insider Tip: Make your tour reservations at least 2 weeks in advance. Total cost: £200-£350 each person. Join group trips to socialize. Perfect for independent adventurers.

ROMANTIC GETAWAYS (3 DAYS)

Ideal for: Couples seeking cozy, picturesque moments.

Overview: This 3-day plan combines romance, scenery, and good meals.

Day 1: Oban Romance

Morning: Stay at Greystones B&B. Stroll along the harbor and get a coffee at The Pokey Hat.

Afternoon: Lunch at Oban Seafood Hut. Visit McCaig's Tower (free).

Evening: Dinner at Ee-Usk (scallops). Evening stroll along Corran Esplanade.

Day 2: Iona

Morning: West Coast Tours to Iona. Explore Iona Abbey.

Afternoon: Picnic on Port Ban Beach. Return by 6 p.m.

Evening: Dinner at Baab (kofta,). Drinks at Cuan Mor.

Day 3 - Ganavan Sands

Morning: Bus to Ganavan Sands. Romantic beach stroll with picnic.

Afternoon: Lunch at The Olive Garden. Depart.

Insider Tip: Book your Iona tour and B&B early. Total cost: £250-£350 per person. Bring a scarf for windy hikes. Perfect for anniversaries or trips.

Wrapping Up

Here's your guide to making the most of Oban, no matter your style! Which itinerary appeals to you, from simple weekend getaways to crazy adventures? Let's keep this Highland expedition going!

CHAPTER 14
DO'S AND DONT'S.

Oban is eager to charm you with its harbors, whiskies, and island vibe, but with a little preparation, your trip can be pleasant and unforgettable. This chapter is your guide to maximizing your visit, whether you're hiking to McCaig's Tower or taking a ferry to Mull. We've got you covered on everything from must-do recommendations to avoidable mistakes, as well as how to respect local culture and the environment. Let's have a look at the do's and don'ts for a stress-free Oban vacation!

Must-Dos for a Great Visit

To make the most of your time in Oban, make a few strategic decisions. These are the must-haves for an unforgettable trip.

Book Ahead for Peak Season: Oban is busy during the summer (June-August), so book your accommodations, ferries, and tours like the Oban Distillery at least 1-2 months in advance. This prevents you from being disappointed by sold-out events, especially on day trips to Mull or Staffa.

Prepare for Scottish Weather: Oban's weather is notoriously unpredictable, sunny one minute, rainy the next. Bring a waterproof jacket, sturdy shoes, and layers, even in the summer. A small umbrella or hat is useful for harbor tours and hikes to Pulpit Hill (Chapter 9).

Try Local Flavors: Dive into Oban's cuisine scene. Oban Seafood Hut serves seafood, while The Lorne Bar offers haggis. To sample Scotland's sweet side, go to Oban Chocolate Company and purchase a tablet.

Explore by Foot: The town's compact center is easily explored on a leisurely stroll. Visit iconic spots like McCaig's Tower and St. Columba's Cathedral to absorb the atmosphere. Pick up a map at the Visitor Information Centre to navigate with ease.

Join a Ceilidh: A ceilidh provides an opportunity to experience Scottish culture (Chapter 10). Check out The Lorne Bar or Corran Halls for live music or dancing evenings. Even just watching provides a wonderful look into local life.

Why do these? These measures guarantee that you see Oban's attractions, stay comfortable, and connect with its heart. They're simple victories for every traveler, from solitary adventurers to families.

Common Mistakes to Avoid

While Oban is forgiving, a few newbie mistakes might trip you up. Avoid these if you want your trip to go smoothly.

Skipping Ferry Reservations: Don't expect you can just show up for ferries to Mull, Iona, or Staffa (Chapter 14). Summer sailings sell out quickly, particularly for cars. Book at calmac.co.uk or staffatours.com 1-2 weeks in advance.

Underestimating Weather: Even if the forecast says it will be sunny, don't forget to carry a raincoat. Oban's coastline environment changes fast; be prepared for showers on Kerrera hikes or frigid winds at Ganavan Sands.

Overpacking Your Day: Oban's laid-back pace is not conducive to hectic schedules. Avoid packing Mull and Iona into one day; it is feasible but tiring. For a more relaxing atmosphere, spread out your island travels across many days.

Ignoring Pub Etiquette: Don't wave money or expect table service in bars like Cuan Mor. Order at the bar, wait for your turn, then say "cheers" when served. It's how the native's roll.

Missing Out on Free Attractions: Don't dismiss free jewels such as the Oban War and Peace Museum or McCaig's Tower because you believe paid sites are superior. These locations, rich in history and scenery, are ideal for budget tourists.

Why Should I Avoid These? Avoiding these blunders saves time, money, and frustration, allowing you to appreciate Oban's beauty.

Cultural Sensitivity and Etiquette

Oban's residents are warm and hospitable, but respecting their culture and traditions goes a long way. Here's how to blend in like an expert.

Be Polite and Patient: Scots value civility, so be kind and patient. Say "please" and "thank you" in shops like Oban Craft Shop and cafés like The Pokey Hat. Don't hurry the servers, Oban's pace is relaxed, especially in pubs.

Respect Gaelic Heritage: Gaelic is visible in Oban through signage ("An t-Òban") and music. Try a term like "Slàinte" (cheers) at The Lorne Bar; locals appreciate the effort. Don't ridicule accents or traditions.

Mind Personal Space: Scots are friendly yet reserved. Don't get into intimate conversations with strangers at a ceilidh or market. A simple grin and conversation about the weather or whisky opens doors.

Dress Appropriately: Casual attire is OK for bars or hikes, but shoulders and knees should be covered in St.

Columba's Cathedral or Iona Abbey. Avoid wearing loud logos or beachwear in cultural settings.

Tip Modestly: Tipping is optional but appreciated. Leave 10-15% if service is not included at eateries such as Ee-Usk. Round up in cafés or bars such as Cuan Mor.

Why Should We Care? These gestures demonstrate respect for Oban's community, making your interactions more genuine.

SAFETY TIPS FOR TRAVELERS

Oban is one of Scotland's safest places, but a few measures may make your trip worry-free, whether you're hiking or pub-hopping.

Stay Weather Aware: Before hikes to Beinn Lora or boat cruises to Staffa, check the weather forecast (metoffice.gov.uk). Storms can hit quickly; postpone if winds surpass 30 mph. Carry a fully charged phone in case of an emergency.

Watch Your Step: When wet, Oban's harbor cobblestones and hilly trails such as Pulpit Hill can become slippery. Wear sturdy shoes and stick to the marked paths. Avoid unlit areas at night, such as the rural road to Ganavan Sands.

Secure Valuables: Oban has a low crime rate, however don't leave baggage unattended in crowded areas like Argyll Square or the ferry port. Passports and cash can be kept inside hotel safes at places like Glenbervie Guest House.

Know Ferry Safety: On ferries to Mull or Kerrera, observe the crew's instructions and use life jackets if provided. Stay seated amid rough seas. Check calmac.co.uk for updates on the weather to avoid cancellations.

Drink Responsibly: Pubs like The Lorne Bar are enjoyable, but avoid drinking too much whiskey or lager. Follow well-lit roads back to your accommodation, such as George Street. Inform someone of your plans if you are traveling alone.

Why Should I Stay Safe? These guidelines help you enjoy Oban's experiences without mistakes, maintaining your focus on the fun.

ENVIRONMENTAL RESPONSIBILITY

Oban's natural beauty, its beaches, islands, and wildlife, is important, and responsible tourism helps conserve it for future visitors. Here's how to tread softly.

Leave No Trace: Do not trash along paths like Kerrera or beaches like Ganavan Sands. Trash should be placed in containers or packed out. Avoid plucking plants or damaging stones at locations such as Kilmartin Glen.

Support Eco-Friendly Businesses: Choose companies like Sea Kayak Oban that use sustainable techniques, or eateries like Food from Argyll that use local products. Purchase gifts from shops such as The Jetty Gallery, which showcases eco-conscious artists.

Minimize Plastic: Bring a reusable water bottle and a tote bag to markets or picnics. Avoid single-use plastics at the Oban Farmers' Market; exhibitors frequently provide eco-friendly alternatives.

Respect Wildlife: On a Staffa or Mull trip, respect wildlife by staying a safe distance from seals and puffins. Use binoculars for looking rather than approaching. Follow the regulations set by the guides on wildlife cruises (Chapter 9).

Walk Or Take Public Transportation: Oban is walkable, and buses to Ganavan Sands or Kilmartin reduce your carbon impact. Rent bikes from Oban Cycles for eco-friendly exploration.

Why Go Green? These initiatives maintain Oban's ecosystems, ensuring that seals, eagles, and beaches survive. Furthermore, communities value tourists who care.

Wrapping Up

That is your map to an unforgettable Oban trip! From scheduling ferries to honoring Gaelic culture and keeping the shore clean, these do's and don'ts will help you succeed. What's your first move: grab a dram or go hiking to a view? Let us make your Oban adventure sparkle!

Chapter 15

PRACTICAL INFORMATION.

Hello, traveler! Are you ready to embrace Oban's coastal charm? Let's go over the details that will make your vacation as smooth as a Highland breeze. This chapter covers all you need to know about money, keeping connected, and preparing for Scotland's unpredictable weather. Whether you're exploring George Street or hiking Kerrera, these ideas can help you stay prepared and stress-free. Let's take care of the logistics so you can enjoy yourself!

Currency and Payment Options.

Let's talk money, Oban isn't a cash-only landscape, but understanding the payment system allows you to buy, dine, and tip like you know it all.

Currency: The British Pound Sterling (GBP, £) is the currency in Oban, as it is across Scotland. Notes come in denominations of £5, £10, £20, and £50, while coins include 1p, 2p, 5p, 10p, 20p, 50p, £1, and £2. Scottish banks (like the Bank of Scotland) mint its own notes that differ in appearance yet are valid across the United Kingdom. Expect to pay around £5 for a coffee and scone or for a pub dinner.

Payment Options: Contactless cards (Visa, Mastercard, and American Express) are accepted in most establishments in Oban, including hotels like Muthu Alexandra, restaurants like Ee-Usk, and shops like The Jetty Gallery. Apple Pay and Google Pay are also widespread. Smaller establishments, such as Oban Seafood Hut or market booths, may be cash-only, particularly for transactions. ATMs are available on George Street and in Tesco, with no costs for UK cards (check with your bank to enquire about foreign card fees).

Insider Tips: Carry £20-£30 in cash for small purchases or tips (10-15% at restaurants). Banks and the Oban Post Office provide better currency exchange rates than airports do. Notify your bank of your trip plans to avoid card bans. If you are given Scottish notes, don't be concerned, they are legal currency, however some English shops may hesitate (few in Oban). Budget tourists should use card payments to simply track their expenditures.

INTERNET AND MOBILE CONNECTIVITY

Whether you're taking harbor pictures or driving to McCaig's Tower, being connected in Oban is a breeze. Here's an overview of Wi-Fi and mobile connectivity possibilities.

Wi-Fi: Free Wi-Fi is available at Oban's hotels (Greystones B&B), cafés (The Pokey Hat), and bars (Cuan Mor). The Visitor Information Centre on North Pier also provides free Wi-Fi. Speeds are enough for surfing or streaming, however rural locations such as Kerrera may have intermittent service. Public Wi-Fi in Argyll Square is accessible but sluggish.

Oban has reliable 4G coverage from major UK providers (EE, O2, Vodafone, and Three). 5G is limited, but expanding. Signal drops on ferries to Staffa and distant trails such as Beinn Lora. EU tourists benefit from roaming plans (check with your carrier), while others need obtain a UK SIM card at Tesco or Oban Mobile Shop on George Street. A 10GB prepaid SIM card costs between £10 and £20 for 30 days.

Insider Tip: For hikes or islands, get offline maps (such as Maps.me). Save data by uploading via Wi-Fi. Keep your phone powered on lengthy trips by carrying a portable charger. Tag #VisitOban in your social media posts to show your support for the local community. For solo travelers, communicate your itinerary over WhatsApp to ensure safety.

Local Time Zone and Business Hours.

Timing is key in Oban, from catching ferries to getting a late-night pint. Let us break down the time and schedules.

Time Zone: Oban follows Greenwich Mean Time (GMT) from October to March, then British Summer Time (GMT+1) from April to September. Clocks will be set forward in April 2025, so update your watch if you travel across time zones.

Business Hours: Shops on George Street (e.g., Oban Craft Shop, Chapter 13) are normally open from 9 a.m. to 5 p.m., with some extending until 6 p.m. in summer. Cafes like Food from Argyll are open from 8 a.m. to 4 p.m., while restaurants like Piazza are open until 9-10 p.m. Pubs such as The Lorne Bar are open till midnight or 1 a.m. Attractions such as Dunollie Castle are typically open from 10 a.m. to 4 p.m., April through October. Sunday hours may be shortened (noon to 4 p.m. for shops). Ferries to Mull or Kerrera run from 7 a.m. to 6 p.m., with reduced winter schedules.

Insider Tips: Check calmac.co.uk for ferry schedules and whatsonoban.com for event hours. To avoid crowds, plan your visits to attractions for midweek. Arrive 10 minutes early for scheduled tours such as Oban Walking tours. If you are jet-lagged, consider an evening harbor stroll to help you acclimate.

Healthcare and Medical Services

Oban is a secure place, but knowing where to go for medical help keeps you worry-free, whether it's a scratched knee or a misplaced prescription.

Medical Services: Lorn and Islands Hospital (Glengallan Road, a 10-minute walk from the harbor) includes a 24-hour emergency room (NHS, free to UK residents). EU travelers use EHIC cards, while others require travel insurance (check coverage). For mild issues (colds, wounds), go to Lorn Medical Centre (George Street, 8 a.m.-6 p.m., appointments required). Boots Pharmacy (George Street) sells over-the-counter medications and fills prescriptions (bring your script).

Health Tips: Tap water is safe to drink; refill in cafeterias. There are no severe health dangers in Oban, however midges (biting insects) can be annoying in the summer; buy repellent at stalls. When hiking Pulpit Hill or kayaking, bring a basic first-aid kit (plasters, antiseptic). Food hygiene is high in restaurants like Oban Seafood Hut, so wash your hands before eating.

Insider Tips: Bring adequate medication for your trip, boots might aid in an emergency. Call 999 for emergency treatment or 111 for non-emergency assistance. Obtain travel insurance for peace of mind, particularly for active holidays like Staffa. Families, take note of the hospital's kid-friendly services.

PACKING TIP FOR OBAN'S CLIMATE

Oban's weather is notoriously unpredictable; sun, rain, and wind might all fall in one day. Packing carefully makes you comfortable whether you're visiting Ganavan Sands or Iona Abbey.

Essentials:

Waterproof Jackets and Shoes: Hikes to Kerrera and ferry rides require a lightweight raincoat and strong, waterproof boots (Chapter 14). It's preferable to use Gore-Tex or something comparable.

Layers: Bring breathable shirts, a fleece, and a scarf for cool evenings (even in July, lows can reach 10°C/50°F). Thermals are beneficial for winter trips.

Accessories: A little umbrella, hat, and sunglasses cover all bases. Bring a daypack for picnics and gifts from the Oban Farmers' Market.

Extras: A reusable water bottle and tote bag are environmentally appropriate for markets or cafés. Binoculars improve wildlife expeditions to Staffa.

Seasonal Notes: Summer in Oban (June to August) brings mild temperatures (15-20°C/60-68°F), but expect rain. Be sure to pack layers for your visit. Winter (November-March) is cooler (5-10°C/40-50°F) with shorter days; wear gloves and thick clothing. Spring and fall wardrobes should be adaptable.

Insider Tips: To conserve space, mix & match clothing. Check metoffice.gov.uk before leaving. Leave your nice shoes at home, the cobblestones of North Pier are merciless. If you're flying, put items in your carry-on in case luggage is delayed.

Visa & Entry Requirements

Oban is a part of the United Kingdom, so requirements for entry are uncomplicated, but it's worth double-checking to prevent surprises at the border.

Visa Rules: EU/EEA, US, Canadian, Australian, and many other nationalities do not require a visa to visit the UK for up to 6 months (for tourism purposes only). Check gov.uk to see what your country's status is. Others (e.g., India and China) require a Standard Visitor Visa (£100, apply three months ahead). Passports must be valid for the duration of your stay; there is no minimum validity beyond that.

Entry Process: If you arrive by air (Glasgow/Edinburgh) or rail (Eurostar), you should expect passport inspections. If questioned, have your hotel details (for example, Greystones B&B) and return plans available.

Customs: Allows you to transport 1L of spirits (e.g., Oban whisky, 200 cigarettes, and £390 in goods duty-free. If entering non-EU countries, declare foods such as smoked salmon and verify the destination laws. No monetary declaration is required until the amount exceeds £10,000.

Insider Tips: Apply for a visa as soon as possible through gov.uk. Photocopy your passport and keep it separate. For healthcare, EU tourists need hold an EHIC. There are no additional inspections required while visiting Mull; UK regulations apply to everybody. Share entrance information with family members if you're traveling alone.

Wrapping Up

That's it, your practical guide to rocking Oban! From pounds to packing, visas to Wi-Fi, you're ready for a smooth journey. What comes next? booking the ferry or choosing your pub? Let's keep the Oban adventure going!

Chapter 16

FAMILY-FRIENDLY ACTIVITIES

Hello, parents! Planning a trip with the kids to Oban? You're in for a treat; this coastal treasure has activities for the entire family, from toddlers to teenagers. Consider interactive museums, sandy beaches, and boat trips where you may see a seal or two. Whether you're looking for adventure or a quiet lunch for the whole family, this chapter is your guide to family-friendly activities in Oban. Let's get into the best strategies to make your trip a success with the kids!

Child-Friendly Attractions and Museums

Oban's attractions and museums are jam-packed with hands-on activities that will pique kids' interest while also entertaining adults.

What's On Offer? Oban's museums are small but interesting, featuring displays that bring local history to life. Most are conveniently located, inexpensive, and quick to visit, making them perfect for people with short attention spans. Expect entry costs of £0-£8, and many are stroller-friendly.

Top Picks:

Oban War and Peace Museum: This volunteer-run jewel features kid-friendly displays such as vintage uniforms, model boats, and WWII memorabilia. Kids enjoy the hands-on activities, such as stroking a sailor's cap. It takes 30-60 minutes and is appropriate for children aged five and above.

Dunollie Museum (near Dunollie Castle): This museum is a 15-minute walk from town and examines the MacDougall clan with costumes, ancient toys, and a weaving shed where kids may try the looms. The castle grounds are ideal for exploration. Recommended for ages 6 to 12.

Why Should You Visit? These attractions combine education and entertainment, keeping kids interested while parents learn about Oban. They are affordable and conveniently located near eateries for food breaks.

Insider Tip: Visit midweek to avoid crowds. Ask the staff about kid-friendly activities, Dunollie hosts scavenger hunts. Bring a lightweight jacket for the chilly museum rooms. Combine with a harbor stroll (Chapter 12) for a full morning.

Outdoor Play Spaces and Parks

Oban's outdoor areas are ideal for families, with beaches, playgrounds, and green places where kids may play while parents enjoy the scenery.

What's Available? Oban's outdoor spaces, from sandy beaches to grassy parks, are free, safe, and ideal for picnics and fun. Most are a short walk or bus ride from the center, with amenities such as benches and bathrooms.

Top Spots:

Ganavan Sands (2 miles north): This golden beach is a popular family destination for sandcastle building, paddling, and rockpool finding. There is a small playground with picnic tables. Great for all ages, with amazing views of Mull. Bring a bucket and spade.

Atlantis Leisure Park (Dalriach Road; 10-minute walk): This park, located next to the Atlantis Leisure Center, features swings, slides, and a climbing frame for children aged 3 to 12. Grass nearby is ideal for frisbee or kite flying. Toilets are free and located in the center.

Why Go? While parents relax in gorgeous settings, kids may run wild in these areas. They are affordable and adaptable to any schedule, making them great for after a museum visit.

Insider Tips: Bring sunscreen and caps to Ganavan because the sun is intense in the summer. Bring a picnic (£5-10) from Food from Argyll. Check the tide timings at Ganavan to maximize beach area. Spend the entire day in Atlantis Park, either before or after a swim at the leisure facility.

Family Boat Trips & Tours.

Nothing screams adventure like a boat trip, and Oban's family-friendly alternatives provide wildlife, beauty, and entertainment for all ages.

What's Out There? Short boat trips departing from Oban's harbor are created with kids in mind and focus on seals, birds, and island vistas. Prices range from £15 and £50 per person, with reductions available for children under the age of 12. Trips take 1-3 hours, making things manageable for children.

Top Picks:

Seafari Adventures (North Pier, £25/adult, £15/child): These 2-hour wildlife tour cruise around the Firth of Lorn, watching seals, porpoises, and seabirds. Kids receive binoculars while guides give interesting things. Recommended for ages 4 and above.

Kerrera Ferry and Walk (Gallanach): A 15-minute boat ride to Kerrera allows families to explore accessible coastal walks and view sheep and seals. The Kerrera Tea Garden serves kid-friendly food (£5). Ideal for ages 6 and up.

Why Try It? Boat trips are an exciting way to view Oban's marine life, and guides keep kids engaged. They're short enough to avoid boredom yet crammed with memorable moments.

Insider Tips: Book Seafari at least a week in advance (seafari.co.uk). Sea breezes might be cool, so dress kids in layers. Bring a small toy or book to pass the time while waiting for the ship. Check the weather; severe waves might cause trips to be cancelled. Combine with lunch at Oban Seafood Hut for a harbor-themed day.

Workshops and Interactive Experiences.

Kids can get creative with Oban's workshops and hands-on activities, which range from painting to history and provide enjoyable learning opportunities for the entire family.

What's Happening? Local establishments host kid-friendly activities, which are themed around Oban's culture or crafts. These are small-scale, inexpensive, and ideal for rainy days or curious minds. Check the schedules at whatsonoban.com.

Top Experiences:

Dunollie Museum Weaving Workshop (Aged 6 and up): Children may practice hand-weaving or make little tartan crafts while learning about Highland traditions. Sessions (1-2 hours) take place during the summer or at events such as the Oban Games.

Rockfield Centre Art Classes (Stevenson Street): This community arts hub provides drop-in painting and pottery classes for kids, with take-home masterpieces. Best for children aged 4 to 12, with 1-hour sessions.

Why Should You Join? Kids explore Oban's culture via these activities, which also provide them with souvenirs to display. Parents can participate or relax nearby.

Tips: Book classes a few days in advance at dunollie.org or rockfieldcentre.org.uk. Aprons are recommended for art lessons since things can become dirty. Combine with a visit to The Jetty Gallery for further crafting ideas. Search for festival seminars in August or November.

DINING OPTIONS FOR FAMILIES

Oban's dining culture is surprisingly kid-friendly, with restaurants and cafés that cater to families.

What's Cooking? Expect inexpensive, informal restaurants offering kids' menus, high seats, and friendly service. Many are on George Street or near the harbor, making them convenient for visiting attractions.

Top Spots:

Piazza (North Pier): This Italian restaurant provides kid-sized pizzas and pastas and offers harbor views to keep everyone pleased. Crayons and coloring pages are an added treat. Ideal for ages 2 to 12.

Cuan Mor (George Street): A brewery offering a kids' menu (Fish fingers) and outside sitting in the summer.

The easygoing atmosphere appeals to families, and sweets such as sticky toffee pudding (£6) are popular. Ideal for all ages.

Insider Tips: Reserve a table at Piazza for dinner (summer gets hectic). Request lesser quantities for finicky eaters at Food from Argyll. Visit early (5-6 p.m.) to escape the pub throng. Bring a small toy to keep children engaged. Oban Chocolate Company serves hot cocoa.

Wrapping Up

That's it; your guide to a family-friendly Oban adventure! What's first on your kids' must-do list, from splashing at Ganavan Sands to weaving in Dunollie? Let's make this trip a blast for the entire team!

Chapter 17

FESTIVALS AND EVENTS

Hello, festival fan! Oban's calendar is jam-packed with events that bring this coastal town to life, like kilted Highland games, yacht-filled harbors, and festive winter markets. Whether you're cheering on caber tossers, eating fresh seafood, or dancing at a ceilidh, these events highlight Oban's lively culture and community spirit. This chapter delves into the key events, such as the renowned Oban Games, West Highland Yachting Week, Oban Seafood Festival, and Winter Festival, as well as tips for securing tickets and planning your trip. Let us prepare to join the party!

Oban Games: Highland Traditions.

The Oban Games, also known as the Argyllshire Gathering, are a must-see if you want to feel Scotland's Highland spirit. This day-long event at Mossfield

Stadium, held every year on the last Thursday of August, is a colorful celebration of heritage.

What's the Vibe? Picture kilts whirling, bagpipes skirling, and athletes tossing cabers (tree trunks weighing up to 130 pounds!). The Games, which attract contestants and tourists from all over the world, comprise of Highland dance, piping competitions, and heavier activities such as hammer throws and tug of war. The March of the Stewards (10:30 a.m. from Station Square) is led by pipers, and the Oban High School Pipe Band performs at noon. The kids enjoy the fun races and the bouncy castle, while history aficionados can learn about Argyll's heritage through exhibitions on clans and piping. Local food stalls sell haggis, shortbread, and whisky. Expect 5,000–10,000 attendees, generating a vibrant vibe.

Why Go? It's a family-friendly, engaging way to see Highland culture up close, Imagine athletic feats, music, and community pride. Ideal for all ages, from toddlers to grandparents.

Insider Tips: Arrive by 9:30 a.m. for the full immersion (ends 4:30 p.m.). Walk from Argyll Square (10–12 minutes) or use public transport, parking's limited to Blue Badge holders. Dress for changing weather (layers, comfy shoes). Bring a picnic or cash for the stalls.

West Highland Yachting Week

If you enjoy the water, West Highland Yachting Week (late July to early August, most likely July) is a stunning event that transforms Oban's harbor into a sailing spectacle. It has been Scotland's largest sailing event for 78 years.

What's Happening? This week-long regatta, held at Oban, Craobh Marina, and Tobermory (Mull), includes competitive racing from passage races to Olympic-style courses, and attracts up to 200 yachts. On land, family enjoy a carnival atmosphere complete with live music, picnics, and ceilidhs, particularly at Corran Halls for the prize-giving ceremony. The Tunnock's Fleet (spinnaker classes) and Argyll Fleet (limited sail) make it accessible to both pros and beginners, including kids who race as crew members. Shore-based tourists can watch races from Oban's North Pier or attend post-sail events such as live bands.

Why Attend? It's a wonderful blend of sport and socializing, with Oban's harbor gleaming with sails. Ideal for families, couples, or sailing enthusiasts seeking a joyful atmosphere.

Insider Tips: For the most recent schedule, visit whyw.co.uk. Oban fills up quickly, so book your accommodations early. Bring binoculars for race viewing and a jacket for windy evenings. There are no tickets required for shore events, but budget between £10 and £20 for food and beverages. If you're visiting Tobermory, pair it with a Mull Day trip.

OBAN SEAFOOD FESTIVAL

Calling all foodies! The Oban Seafood Festival (usually in mid-September) commemorates Oban's status as Scotland's Seafood hub with a weekend of fresh catches and gastronomic delights.

What's Cooking? This event, held around the port and Argyll Square, offers stalls selling scallops, langoustines, smoked salmon, and fish and chips. While kids enjoy face painting and seafood-themed crafts, local chefs from locales like Ee-Usk give cooking demonstrations. Live music, ranging from folk to pipers, fills the air, and visitors can drink local ales or Oban whiskey. Expect sustainable fishing demonstrations as well as sampling of Argyll cheeses and tablets. It's a relaxing, food-focused gathering with 3,000-5,000 attendees.

Why Should You Join? It's a delightful opportunity to sample Oban's marine riches while enjoying the waterfront views and local music. Ideal for families and food-loving couples.

Insider Tips: Check whatsonoban.com for upcoming events dates. Arrive early (10 a.m.) to get the finest stall options to choose from. Bring cash for smaller sellers; most accept cards. Wear comfortable shoes when standing and sampling. Combine with a visit to Oban Distillery for a food and drink experience.

Winter Festival and Christmas Events.

When winter shows up, Oban brightens up with the Oban Winter Festival (November - December), a month-long festival of holiday cheer ideal for families and warm vibes.

What's The Deal? The celebration takes place in places such as Argyll Square, Corran Halls, and the harbor, and includes Victorian Markets selling handcrafted items, local cheeses, and mulled wine. The Reindeer Parade and Christmas Lights Switch-On (late November) are popular among children, with Santa and the Oban Pipe Band taking center stage. Corran Halls showcases Gaelic music, fiddle performances, and ceilidhs (from £10 to £20), while lantern parades and fire art illuminate the streets. Other attractions include Distillery Markets with food vendors and Hogmanay celebrations (December 31) at pubs such Cuan Mor. The joyful mood attracts almost 5,000 guests.

Why Go? It's a pleasant way to experience Oban's community spirit, complete with family-friendly activities and romantic moments beneath shimmering lights.

Insider Tips: For the years program, check obanwinterfestival.com. Dress warmly, November evenings drop below 5°C (40°F). Book your Corran Halls tickets early; markets are free. Stay close to the harbor for quick access. Visit during the week when there are less crowds.

BOOK TICKETS AND PLAN AHEAD

A little planning goes a long way when it comes to enjoying Oban's festivals. Here's how to secure your spot and prepare like a professional.

Oban Games: Tickets are available at obangames.com or on the day at Mossfield Stadium (cash/card accepted). Book online before mid-August to avoid gate lineups. Check the schedule for major events, such as the Hill Race. To minimize parking issues, arrive by public transport (10-minute walk from Station Square; travelinescotland.com).

West Highland Yachting Week: Most shore events are free, although ceilidhs or dinners require tickets from whyw.co.uk. Book Oban hotels (e.g., Greystones B&B) before May, since yachting week fills up quickly. Check social media (@WestHighlandYachtingWeek) for pop-up activities. If you plan to race, please register before June.

Oban Seafood Festival: Entry is free, however bring £20-£50 for food and beverages. Check whatsonoban.com or visitscotland.com for verified 2025 dates (announced in spring). For festival weekends, make reservations a week in advance at seafood restaurants such as Piazza.

Winter Festival: Markets and parades are free; book Corran Halls performances or ceilidhs at obanwinterfestival.com by October. Hogmanay activities at pubs may require reservations; check with The Lorne Bar. Stay informed with the festival's newsletter.

General Tips:

Book Early: Oban's festivals draw crowds, so plan accommodation and event tickets 1–3 months ahead, especially for August and November. Use oban.org.uk to find listings.

Check The Weather: Bring clothes and waterproofs for outdoor events such as the Games or yachting week. Umbrellas are useful for winter marketplaces.

Plan Transportation: Ferries to Mull during yachting week and busses to Mossfield Stadium require booking ahead (calmac.co.uk, westcoastmotors.co.uk). To avoid parking issues, walk or bike all through town.

Budget Smart: Expect to spend between £50-£100 each day on festival food, beverages, and tickets. Save money by picnicking or attending free events such as parades.

Stay Flexible: Weather might change plans, so have indoor alternatives like Oban Phoenix Cinema for wet festival days.

Why Plan? Early booking and careful planning ensure that you get the finest places and can enjoy Oban's celebrations without hassle, whether you're dancing at a ceilidh or savoring scallops.

Wrapping Up

There you have an Oban's festival roster, ready to enhance your trip with Highland flare! From cabers to yachts, reindeer to whiskey, what event has your name on it? Let's begin planning and have some fun!

Chapter 18

SUSTAINABLE TRAVEL IN OBAN

Hello, eco-warrior! Oban's stunning beaches, wildlife, and Highland flair are worth saving, and vacationing responsibly allows you to enjoy this treasure while preserving its beauty. This chapter is your guide to exploring Oban while being environmentally conscious, from staying in green hotels to supporting local artists and reducing your carbon impact. Whether you're drinking coffee in a zero-waste cafe or biking to Ganavan Sands, these tips will help you make a difference. Let's look at how to get to Oban in a green way!

Eco-Friendly Accommodation and Dining

Oban has an increasing number of eco-friendly places to stay and eat, making it simple to select options that promote sustainability without sacrificing comfort or flavor.

Accommodation: Look for accommodations with green credentials, such as energy-efficient systems or local sourcing. Greystones B&B on Dalriach Road has solar panels, recycles waste, and provides organic breakfasts. Oban Glamping (near Ganavan Sands) provides low-impact pods with composting toilets and rainwater harvesting. Both are family-run, which reduces corporate waste. Oban Youth Hostel adopts SYHA's eco-friendly practices, such as LED lighting and recycling.

Dining: Oban's restaurants prioritize local, sustainable food. Food from Argyll (Argyll Square) is a deli-cafe that sells Argyll cheeses, smoked salmon, and organic vegetables. Cuan Mor (George Street) employs seasonal, locally sourced fish and manufactures its own beer, reducing transportation emissions (£12-20). The Pokey Hat (George Street) provides vegan and gluten-free alternatives in biodegradable packaging (£4–£8). These locations promote zero-waste methods and assist local farmers.

Why Should You Choose These? Eco-friendly lodging and dining lessen your environmental impact while supporting Oban's green economy. Furthermore, the cuisine is fresher, and the housing seems real.

Insider Tips: Book eco-lodges through green-tourism.com or direct websites. Inquire with restaurants regarding sourcing food from Argyll. Bring a reusable coffee cup to the café for discounts (10-20%). Look for vegan options at Cuan Mor to reduce your impact.

SUPPORTING LOCAL BUSINESS

Oban's local businesses, artisans, retailers, and tour operators are the heart of the community, and your purchases can assist them thrive while preserving the town's distinct flair.

What's Out There? Avoid chain retailers and instead visit independent establishments. The Jetty Gallery (George Street) sells seascapes and ceramics by Argyll artists for between £20 and £500, therefore supporting creatives. Oban Craft Shop (Stafford Street) sells handwoven tartans and whiskey barrel crafts by local craftsmen. Sea Kayak Oban offers eco-friendly tours with local guides. Oban Farmers' Market (Argyll Square, first Saturday of each month) is a goldmine for local cheeses, tablets, and knitwear (£5-£20).

Why Should I Support Them? Small businesses retain money in Oban, preserving its identity and lowering the carbon footprint of imported items. You'll also be able to collect one-of-a-kind souvenirs and hear stories from enthusiastic owners.

Insider Tips: Look for the "Made in Scotland" label at Oban Craft Shop. Talk to sellers at the farmers' market; they usually give eco-tips. Avoid third-party costs by booking tours directly with companies such as Sea Kayak Oban. Bring cash to markets, since some stalls accept cash only. Visit throughout the week to avoid crowds and meet shops.

Reducing Your Environmental Impact

Oban's beautiful beaches and wildlife flourish when visitors tread softly. Small adjustments in your behavior might have a tremendous impact on the surrounding ecology.

How To Do It:

Reduce Waste: Avoid single-use plastics by bringing a reusable water bottle and tote bag while shopping at The Pokey Hat or Oban Seafood Hut. On walks to Pulpit Hill or Kerrera, use garbage cans or carry out your rubbish.

Conserve Resources: Shorten showers at Oban Glamping to conserve water. Turn off the lights and disconnect the charges in your room. Calmac.co.uk offers digital tickets for ferries to Mull.

Respect Nature: To conserve the vegetation, stick to the signposted trails at Ganavan Sands or Beinn Lora. Keep a 50-meter distance from seals and puffins on Staffa tours (Chapter 14). Avoid plucking plants or disturbing stones in Kilmartin Glen.

Eat Locally: To reduce food miles, order seasonal meals at Cuan Mor (for example, local scallops, £20). Avoid foreign meats and tropical fruits in stores.

Why Does It Matter? These methods protect Oban's ecosystems, from the sea life to the highlands, ensuring that future visitors may experience the same beauty. Locals' welcome visitors who respect their house.

Tips: Buy eco-friendly toiletries at Boots (George Street). Download the Refill app for water bottle stations. If you're visiting during the Oban Seafood Festival, help clean up the beach. Pack food in reusable containers for picnics.

Volunteering and Community Initiatives.

Do you want to give back to Oban? Even if you just have a short stay, volunteering or participating in community projects allows you to interact with people while also supporting conservation.

Opportunities:

Beach Clean-ups: Oban Sea Life Sanctuary, Argyll Coast and Islands Hope Spot organizes cleanups at Ganavan Sands and Dunollie. Monthly sessions (1-2 hours long, free) are held, typically in conjunction with festivities such as the Winter Festival. Gloves and bags are provided; register at hopespot.scot.

Community Events: Volunteer at the Oban Farmers' Market or Winter Festival to assist with stalls or children's activities (2-4 hours, free). For more information about positions, visit obanwinterfestival.com. Ideal for families and lone travelers.

Wildlife Monitoring: Sea Life Adventures periodically recruits volunteers to report seal and dolphin sightings on Seil Island cruises for a £10 payment. Check sealife-adventures.co.uk for available options.

Why Volunteer? You will meet people, learn about Oban's ecology, and make a good impact. It's a wonderful way to make your vacation more meaningful, especially for eco-conscious tourists.

Insider Tip: To participate in clean-ups or activities, email organizers 2-3 weeks in advance. Wear durable shoes and bring a water bottle. There is no requirement for experience; simply being enthusiastic would suffice. Combine with a visit to the Dunollie Museum to get context for local heritage. Short on time? Instead, donate £5 to £10 to organizations such as Hope Spot.

Green Transport Options

Walking, bicycling, and taking public transportation are all great ways to reduce your carbon footprint while enjoying the landscape in Oban.

Options:

Walking: Oban's compact Centre is ideal for wandering. It takes 5-15 minutes to walk to McCaig's Tower, St. Columba's Cathedral, or The Lorne Bar. It is free, picturesque, and eco-friendly.

Biking: Rent a bike at Oban Cycles (George Street) and cycle to Ganavan Sands (10 minutes) or Dunollie Castle (5 minutes). The cycle tracks are level and safe.

Public Transportation: West Coast Motors buses (westcoastmotors.co.uk) connect Oban to Ganavan , Seil Island, and Kilmartin Glen. Clean, efficient, and cheaper than vehicle rentals.

CalMac ferries to Mull or Kerrera have lower emissions than private boats. To reduce effect, get foot passenger tickets.

Why Go Green? These choices decrease emissions, relieve traffic on Oban's tiny streets, and allow you to take in the scenery at your leisure. In addition, they are reasonably priced.

Insider Tip: Use the West Coast Motors app to get discounts on bus tickets. Book ferry tickets online (calmac.co.uk) to save paper waste. When cycling, be sure to wear the helmet. Check bus schedules, services stop after 6 p.m. For longer visits, such as Inveraray, take a guided tour to share transportation.

Wrapping Up

That concludes your guide to sustainable tourism in Oban! How will you go green, from eco-lodges to beach cleanups and coastal biking? Let us keep Oban's beauty alive and make your trip one for the earth!

Chapter 19

PLAN YOUR TRIP

Hello, traveler! Are you ready to discover Oban's harbors, islands, and Highland charm? Whether you're interested in sampling seafoods, hiking hills, or island-hopping to Mull, a little planning can help your trip run well. This chapter is your guide to planning the ideal Oban vacation, from creating an itinerary to packing wisely and keeping safe. Let's get into the fundamentals for making your trip memorable and stress-free!

Making a Personalized Itinerary

Oban has something for everyone; history enthusiasts, foodies, explorers, and families, so structuring an itinerary is essential for completing your must-sees without feeling hurried.

How to Start: First, decide on your trip length (2-7 days) and vibe. Want to spend a short weekend exploring McCaig's Tower and hiking in Kerrera? Try Weekend Getaway. Craving culture, including ceilidhs and Dunollie Castle? Go for Cultural Immersion. Outdoor enthusiasts may visit Staffa and Beinn Lora with the Adventure plan. Families should review the Family-Friendly Trip. List your top three priorities: seafood at Ee-Usk, a day trip to Mull, or a visit to the Winter Festival.

Building The Plan: Follow A Daily Framework:

Morning: Begin with an attraction or activity (e.g., Oban Distillery tour, £15; ferry to Iona. To avoid congestion, arrive between 9 and 11 a.m.

Afternoon: Plan a relaxing break at Ganavan Sands (free) or lunch at The Pokey Hat. Include downtime for children or jet lag.

Evening: Plan supper (for example, Cuan Mor) and a low-key activity, such as a harbor stroll or live music at The Lorne Bar.

Sample (3 days):

Day 1: Oban Distillery, lunch at Oban Seafood Hut, Dunollie Museum, and supper at Piazza.

Day 2: Ferry to Kerrera, climb to Gylen Castle, lunch at Food from Argyll, and supper at Ee-Usk.

Day 3: Visit Ganavan Sands, spend £20 at Oban Craft Shop, and then go.

Insider Tips: See Chapter 13 for comprehensive itineraries. Use whatsonoban.com to find festival dates. Allow 1-2 hours of buffer time each day for weather or ferry delays. To maintain balance, lone travelers should alternate between group tours and solo hikes.

BOOK TOURS AND ACTIVITIES

Tours and activities in Oban, such as whiskey tastings, wildlife tours, and island hopping, sell out quickly, especially during the summer. Booking beforehand secures your position.

Key Activities:

Oban Distillery Tours: Book 1-2 weeks in advance at obanwhisky.com for summer dates.

Island Day Trips: Mull (ferry), Iona (tour), or Staffa (April-October) at calmac.co.uk or staffatours.com. Reserve at least 2-3 weeks in advance.

Wildlife Cruises: For seals and dolphins, choose Seafari Adventures or Sea Life Adventures. Book 1-2 weeks in advance at seafari.co.uk.

Cultural Tours: include Oban Walking Tours and Dunollie Museum Workshops. Visit obanwalkingtours.co.uk or dunollie.org.

Booking: Use official websites or go to the Visitor Information Centre (North Pier) for in-person assistance. CalMac's app is useful for using ferries. West Coast Tours offers group tours that include Mull and Iona, saving you time planning, book at westcoasttours.co.uk. Pay by card for convenience; some smaller companies accept cash.

Insider Tips: Confirm reservations 48 hours in advance. Check cancelation policies, weather sometimes prevent boat trips. Book an early time for calmer waters or quieter trails. Families might inquire about kid discounts (typically 50% off). Budget tourists should avoid expensive tours in favor of free treks like Pulpit Hill.

Travel Insurance and Safety

Oban is safe; however, travel insurance and simple measures gives peace of mind, particularly for active trips or international tourists.

Insurance: Get protection against medical crises, trip cancellations, and misplaced luggage. Expect to pay between £20 and £50 for a week's policy (for example, World Nomads or Allianz). EU visitors must carry an EHIC card to access the NHS at Lorn and Islands Hospital. Non-EU visitors must have hospital insurance (often between £150 and £500 for basic care). Include adventure coverage for kayaking and hiking.

Safety Tips:

Weather: Before embarking on walks (Beinn Lora) or ferries (Staffa), visit metoffice.gov.uk. Postpone if winds surpass 30 mph.

Navigation: Get offline maps (Maps.me) for rural locations like Kerrera. Carry a charged phone; 999 for emergencies, and 111 for non-urgent assistance.

Valuables: For passports, use the hotel safes at Greystones B&B. Avoid flashing cash in public areas such as Argyll Square.

After a night out at the pub, stick to well-lit walkways like George Street or North Pier. Share your plans with other solo travelers.

Insider Tips: Purchase travel insurance before to trip. Photocopy your passport and keep it separate. Keep the Lorn Medical Centre phone number (01631 563175) ready. Families, bring a first-aid kit for your children's scrapes.

Packing Checklist

Oban's climate and activities necessitate thoughtful packing, whether you're seeing Ganavan Sands or attending a ceilidh at Corran Halls.

Essentials:

Clothing: Waterproof jacket, robust boots, and layers (fleece, breathable tops) for 5-20°C (40-68°F) temperatures. Pack a scarf for the windy ferries (Mull). Casual dress is appropriate for bars such as The Lorne Bar; include one smart outfit for Ee-Usk.

Accessories: Such as a reusable water bottle, an Oban Farmers' Market tote bag, and a small umbrella. Binoculars for Staffa Wildlife. A daypack for hiking or picnicking.

Phone charger, portable battery, and UK plug adaptor (Type G) for non-UK visitors. Download the CalMac and Maps.me applications.

Documents: Like a passport, insurance information, and booking confirmations (digital or physical). If you live in the EU, you'll need an EHIC card.

Seasonal Notes: Summer (June-August) requires sunscreen and a hat; winter (November-March) need thermals and gloves. Spring/autumn (April 2025) strikes a balance between the two; pack adaptable layers.

Insider Tips: Pack versatile clothes for a carry-on luggage. Leave your heels at home—the cobblestones on North Pier are challenging. Buy eco-toiletries at Boots (George Street, £5) to conserve space. Families should include toys or books during ferry delays.

FINAL TIPS FOR A MEMORABLE STAY.

You're nearly ready for Oban; here are the finishing details to make your trip unforgettable.

Embrace the Pace: Oban's attractiveness stems from its laid-back atmosphere. Allow time for impromptu pauses at The Pokey Hat or a sunset at McCaig's Tower.

Connect With Locals: Chat with the personnel at Cuan Mor or the sellers in Oban Craft Shop. Ask for hidden gems, they may lead you to a calm beach or a secret ceilidh.

Go Green: Support environmentally friendly establishments such as Food from Argyll (Chapter 19), and avoid single-use plastics. To make an even bigger difference, participate in a beach clean-up at Ganavan Sands.

Capture Memories: Take shots at North Pier and Gylen Castle, but put the camera away for events like a Lorne Bar music session. Keep a journal of your best moments, such as seafood, scenery, or a dolphin sighting.

Maintain Flexibility: Weather or ferry delays might disrupt plans. Prepare backup plans for wet days, such as the Oban Phoenix Cinema or the Dunollie Museum.

Why Do These Matter? These ideas combine pragmatism with Oban's passion, ensuring you leave with tales rather than worry. They'll make your trip more enjoyable, whether you're traveling alone or with your family.

Wrapping Up

Here's your roadmap for an incredible Oban experience! What's first on your must-do list, from planning your ideal schedule to packing for rain and dancing at a ceilidh? Let us make this Highland vacation unforgettable!

APPENDIX: YOUR ESSENTIAL OBAN TOOLKIT.

Hello, traveler! This appendix is your go-to resource for making your trip as smooth as a Highland breeze, with useful details to keep you prepared and motivated. From emergency numbers to local phrases and useful addresses, we've got everything you need to traverse Oban like an expert. Whether you're lost on a trail, craving fish and chips, or interested on Gaelic, let us help you prepare for a wonderful adventure!

Emergency Contacts.

Oban is a secure place, but having emergency numbers handy brings peace of mind, whether you're trekking Beinn Lora or sailing to Staffa.

General Emergency (police, fire, ambulance): Dial 999 (free, 24/7). Use in emergency situations such as accidents or crimes.

Non-Emergency Medical Advice (NHS 24): Call 111 (free, 24/7). Call for minor ailments such as colds and sprains.

Police Scotland (non-emergency): 101. Report any missing things or small events.

Lorn and Islands Hospital: 01631 567500 (Glengallan Road, 24/7). For emergency and walk-in care.

Oban Coastguard (Maritime Emergencies): 999. For accidents involving ferries or kayaks.

Oban Police Station: 101 or 01786 289070 (Albany Street, 8 a.m.-5 p.m.). For lost passports and queries.

Visitor Information Center: 01631 563122 (North Pier, 9 a.m.–5 p.m.). For travel emergencies or lost items.

Insider Tip: Save these to your phone. EU passengers utilize EHIC at hospitals; others require insurance. Inform someone about your plans for distant hiking.

Maps and Navigational Tools.

Oban is small but surrounded by islands and trails, thus excellent navigation tools are essential for visiting McCaig's Tower or Kilmartin Glen.

Physical Maps: For detailed trails and islands, get an Ordnance Survey Explorer 376 (Oban & North Argyll) at Waterstones (George Street). The Visitor Information Centre provides complimentary Oban town maps.

Apps: Get Maps.me (free, offline) for Oban's streets and trails, including Pulpit Hill (Chapter 9). Google Maps operates in metropolitan areas but requires data. CalMac Ferries App (free) tracks schedules to Mull or Kerrera.

GPS Tools: A portable GPS, such as the Garmin eTrex (£100), is overkill in town but useful for walks to Beinn Lora or Kerrera. Most cellphones come with offline maps.

Walkhighlands.co.uk offers free trail maps for Ganavan Sands and Gylen Castle. The Visitor Centre's touchscreen kiosks provide route planning.

Insider Tips: Download applications before you arrive because rural Wi-Fi is unreliable. Carry a paper map as a backup; trails may lose service. Tideschart.com provides tide times for seaside walks.

MAP OF OBAN

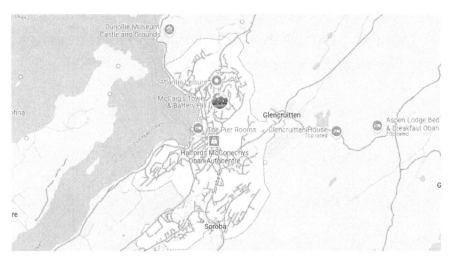

https://maps.app.goo.gl/SYmY72cHy8gpFzpt8

SCAN IMAGE/ QRCODE WITH YOUR PHONE

TO GET THE LOCATION IN REAL TIME

Map of Things to Do

https://maps.app.goo.gl/BZ6RYcm9qZ5eeMb76

SCAN IMAGE/ QRCODE WITH YOUR PHONE

TO GET THE LOCATION IN REAL TIME

Map of Museums

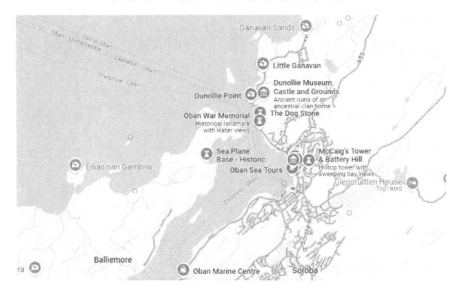

https://maps.app.goo.gl/NuoBd75Yrz6H3H4b6

SCAN IMAGE/
QRCODE
WITH YOUR
PHONE

TO GET THE
LOCATION IN
REAL TIME

Map of Transit Stations

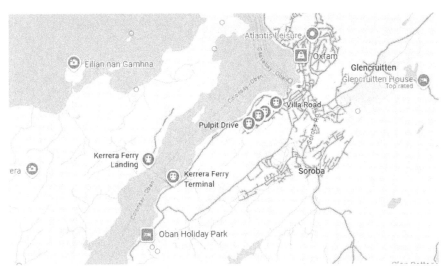

https://maps.app.goo.gl/UjgPgvGziLdPavsv7

SCAN IMAGE/ QRCODE WITH YOUR PHONE

TO GET THE LOCATION IN REAL TIME

Map of Hiking Trails

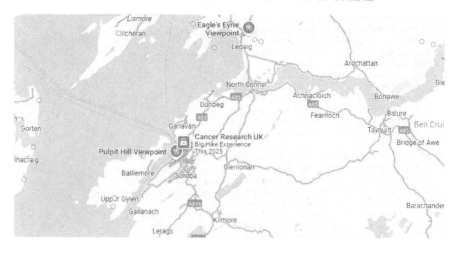

https://maps.app.goo.gl/iJkvwh8kwuB2HMGu9

SCAN IMAGE/ QRCODE WITH YOUR PHONE

TO GET THE LOCATION IN REAL TIME

Map of ATMs

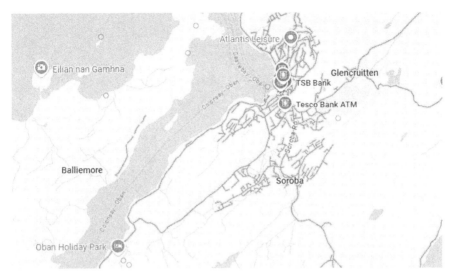

https://maps.app.goo.gl/9p18eHg9NS0ZX5dg7

SCAN IMAGE/
QRCODE
WITH YOUR
PHONE

TO GET THE
LOCATION IN
REAL TIME

Map of Hotels

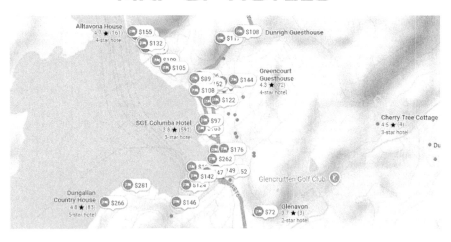

https://maps.app.goo.gl/GT8qgs39LhJZcGWN9

SCAN IMAGE/
QRCODE
WITH YOUR
PHONE

TO GET THE
LOCATION IN
REAL TIME

Map of Restaurants

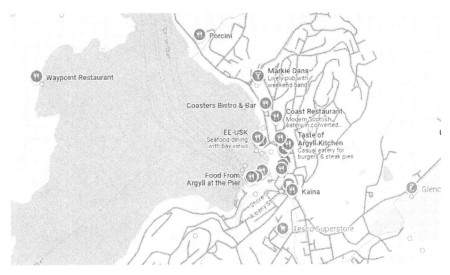

https://maps.app.goo.gl/H27y8J6qNBnLcsuV6

SCAN IMAGE/
QRCODE
WITH YOUR
PHONE

TO GET THE
LOCATION IN
REAL TIME

Map of Vacation Rentals

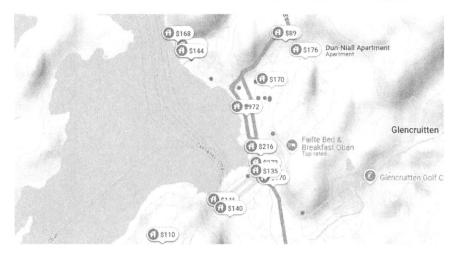

https://maps.app.goo.gl/jYFtjBLWL1J89QGM8

SCAN IMAGE/
QRCODE
WITH YOUR
PHONE

TO GET THE
LOCATION IN
REAL TIME

Additional Reading and References

Want to learn more about Oban's history, culture, and wildlife? These tools will enhance your trip, whether you are planning or reflecting.

Books:

The Oban & Mull Guide by David MacDonald (Waterstones): A concise guide to Oban, Mull, and Iona, complete with history and insider information.

Jim Manthorpe's Scottish Highlands: The Hillwalking Guide is available on Amazon. Includes maps for trails such as Beinn Lora.

The Hebrides by Paul Webster (Waterstones): Stunning photographs and anecdotes of Oban's islands, ideal for Staffa or Iona.

Websites:

VisitScotland.com: Official site for Oban events, hotels, and attractions.

Whatsonoban.com: Local festival and music schedules, including the Oban Games.

Oban.org.uk: A community website with business listings and news.

Blogs/Podcasts:

The Outdoor Diaries (Spotify) has episodes on hiking and kayaking in Argyll.

Buy books at Waterstones in Oban or pre-trip online. Bookmark websites to get real-time updates. Listen to podcasts on the train to Oban (Chapter 7).

Useful Local Phrases.

Oban is primarily English-speaking, although using Gaelic or Scots words adds pleasure and demonstrates appreciation for local culture (Chapter 10). Here's a beginning package.

Gaelic (Gàidhlig): Halò (Hello): Used in Oban Farmers' Market.

Scots/Colloquial:

Aye (Yes): Common at bars such as Cuan Mor.

Wee (small): As in "wee dram" at the Oban Distillery.

Braw (Great): Enhance a view from McCaig's Tower.

Cheers (Thanks): Casual in establishments such as Oban Craft Shop.

Insider Tips: Before your trip, practice your Gaelic with Duolingo's course. Locals appreciate when you try; don't stress about perfection. Get a phrase booklet at the Visitor Information Centre. Use "Slàinte" for Burns Night celebrations.

Addresses and Locations for Popular Accommodation

Oban's housing options range from comfortable bed and breakfasts to inexpensive hostels (Chapter 5). Here are our best recommendations, along with addresses for easy navigating.

Greystones Bed & Breakfast:

Address: Dalriach Road, Oban, PA34 5EQ (5-minute walk from the harbor). Eco-friendly.

Muthu Alexandra Hotel:

Address: Corran Esplanade in Oban, PA34 5AA. Family-friendly.

No.17 The Promenade

Address: 17 Corran Esplanade in Oban, PA34 5AQ and offers coastal views. Boutique.

Oban Youth Hostel:

Address: Esplanade, Oban, PA34 5AF (near the Cathedral). Budget.

Oban Glamping

Address: Gallanachmore Farm, Oban, PA34 4QH (10-minute drive). Eco-pods.

Insider Tips: For the summer, book 1-3 months in advance through oban.org.uk or direct websites. Use Google Maps to validate distances. Greystones and

No.17 are excellent choices for couples, while Muthu is ideal for families.

Addresses and Locations for Popular Restaurants and Cafes

Oban's eating scene is a foodie's paradise, with plentiful fish and pleasant cafés. Here's someplace to eat.

Ee-Usk:

Address: North Pier, Oban, PA34 5QD (harbor front). Seafood (scallops), 12 to 9 p.m.

Cuan Mor:

Address: 60 George Street, Oban, PA34 5SD (central). Brewpub (burger), 11 a.m. to 10 p.m.

Piazza:

Address: North Pier, Oban, PA34 5QD (near to Ee-Usk). Italian (pizza), 12 to 9 p.m.

Oban Seafood Hut

Address: Calmac Pier in Oban, PA34 4DB (the ferry terminus). Fish and chips, 10 a.m. to 6 p.m.

The Pokey Hat

Address: 24 George Street, Oban, PA34 5SB (central). Cafe (scone), 8 a.m. to 4 p.m.

Insider Tips: Make reservations for supper at Ee-Usk or Piazza (01631 565666). Oban Seafood Hut prefers cash transactions. Visit The Pokey Hat early to get fresh pastries. All are walkable from Argyll Square.

ADDRESSES AND LOCATIONS FOR POPULAR BARS AND CLUBS

Oban's nightlife sparkles in its bars, which are ideal for drinks and live music. Clubs are sparse, but bars give.

The Lorne Bar:

Address: Stevenson Street, Oban, PA34 5NA (5-minute walk from the harbor). Traditional pub with live music, 11 a.m. to 1 a.m.

Cuan Mor:

Address: 60 George Street, Oban, PA34 5SD (same as the restaurant). Brewpub with sea views, 11 a.m.–1 a.m.

The View:

Address: 34 George Street, Oban, PA34 5NL (central). Music venue, £5-£8 entry for gigs, 4 p.m.-1 a.m.

Insider Tips: Check The View's Facebook page for concert schedules. To secure a spot, arrive to The Lorne by 8 p.m. Cuan Mor is perfect for couples, whereas Markie Dans is ideal for groups. Walkable from George Street.

ADDRESSES AND LOCATIONS OF MAJOR ATTRACTIONS

Oban's attractions combine history, views, and culture in a readily accessible format.

McCaig's Tower:

Address: Duncraggan Road, Oban, PA34 5AQ (10-minute uphill walk). It is free and open 24 hours a day.

Dunollie Castle and Museum

Address: Dunollie House, Oban, PA34 5TT (15-minute walk). 10 a.m.-4 p.m., April through October.

Oban Distillery:

Address: Stafford Street, Oban, PA34 5NH (central). Book a £15 tour from 10 a.m. to 5 p.m. at obanwhisky.com.

Oban War and Peace Museum

Address: Corran Esplanade in Oban, PA34 5PX (harbor front). Free, 10 a.m.-4 p.m., March-November.

St. Columba's Cathedral

Address: Corran Esplanade in Oban, PA34 5AB (5-minute walk). Free, 9 a.m. to 5 p.m.

Insider Tips: Schedule distillery tours 1-2 weeks in advance. Visit McCaig's Tower at sunset. Dunollie is stroller-friendly, while War and Peace appeals to history aficionados. All are near the North Pier.

Addresses And Locations of Bookstore

Oban's bookstores are ideal for guides, novels, and Gaelic literature.

Waterstones

Address: 12 George Street, Oban, PA34 5SB (central). Maps and travel guides, £5 to £20, 9 a.m. to 5:30 p.m.

Oban Books and Gifts:

Address: 23-25 Stafford Street, Oban, PA34 5NJ (near the distillery). Local history and children's literature, £5 to £15, 10 a.m. to 5 p.m.

Insider Tips: Waterstones carries OS Explorer 376, and Oban Books sells Gaelic phrasebooks. Both accept cards. Walkable from Argyll Square. Midweek is a good time to browse quietly.

Addresses And Locations of Leading Clinics, Hospitals, And Pharmacies.

Oban's healthcare is adequate for minor and urgent requirements.

Lorn and Islands Hospital

Address: Glengallan Road, Oban, PA34 4HH (10-minute walk). Call 01631 567500 for an emergency at any time.

Lorn Medical Centre

Address: Soroba Road, Oban, PA34 4HE (central). GP for mild difficulties, 08 a.m.-6 p.m., 01631 563175.

Boots Pharmacy

Address: 42 George Street, Oban, PA34 5SF (central). Meds and first-aid, £5-10, 9 a.m.-5:30 p.m., 01631 562904.

Insider Tips: Bring your prescription to Boots. To schedule an appointment, call Lorn Medical. The hospital takes EHIC and insurance. Walk or take a cab from George Street.

Addresses and locations of UNESCO World Heritage Sites

Oban has no UNESCO sites, however the adjacent Kilmartin Glen (45-minute drive) is a strong contender for future listing owing to its ancient remains.

Kilmartin Glen (Nether Largie Standing Stones and Dunadd Fort):

Address: Kilmartin, PA31 8RQ (A816). It is free and open 24 hours a day. Kilmartin Museum: Kilmartin, PA31 8RQ; 10 a.m.-5 p.m., kilmartin.org.

Insider Tips: Drive or take the bus (Service 423, westcoastmotors.co.uk). Visit the museum beforehand to gain context. Wear strong shoes, the pathways are uneven. Combine with Seil Island for a day trip.

Wrapping Up

Here's your Oban toolset! You're all set to go, from emergency numbers to bookstores and Gaelic words. What comes first: scheduling a distillery tour or rehearsing "Slàinte"? Let us make this Highland excursion spectacular!

Printed in Dunstable, United Kingdom